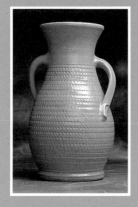

Classic American Pottery

Mitch Tuchman

With a contribution by Jack Chipman

Photographs by **Peter Brenner**

Printed in Hong Kong.

Library of Congress Cataloging-in-Publication
Data available.

ISBN 0-8118-0901-3

Book and cover design: Jim Drobka

Distributed in Canada by Raincoast Books,
8680 Cambie Street, Vancouver, BC V6P 6M9

10 9 8 7 6 5 4 3 2 1

Chronicle Books, 275 Fifth Street
San Francisco, California 94103

*Acknowledgment is due the following for
generously providing photographs:*
PAGE 16 (Bowen Court), courtesy Greene and
Greene Library
PAGES 19 and 47, photos by Edwin Bauer, 1913;
courtesy Dorothy Hilton
PAGE 22, courtesy History Department, Los
Angeles Public Library
PAGE 29, photo, 1946, by Wynn Hammer, then
a student at Art Center College of Design
PAGE 33, photo by Robert Evans, spring 1938
PAGE 50 (Matt Carlton and others), courtesy
Jewell Carlton
PAGE 66, photo by Paul J. Woolf, c. 1934;
courtesy Russel Wright Papers, Department
of Special Collections, Syracuse University
Library
PAGE 104, courtesy Margaret Herrick Library,
Academy of Motion Picture Arts and Sciences

Contents

Preface

They say that in the late 1920s an iconoclastic, young Santa Barbara hostess served dinner to her guests on large, festive J. A. Bauer plant coasters, and there the revolution in colorful, casual dining began. They say that the Bauer family hailed from Atlanta, Georgia, and that the pottery was made at a plant in Pomona, California. They say that the hand-thrown, monumental vases shown in the company's exhibit of art pottery at the Panama-California International Exposition of 1915–16 were the work of a single potter, Matt Carlton, and that the bronze medal awarded the display was a citation of significant esteem. They say that small items were salesmen's samples, that all pieces were actually marked "Bauer," that tablewares were glazed white just once a year, for June weddings. They say that when the company finally folded in 1962, after seventy-seven years in business, the molds for its most popular lines were saved and sold and that Bauer pottery is being manufactured somewhere to this very day, perhaps in Idaho. They say these things, and, of course, they are wrong.

Had they said that the J. A. Bauer Pottery Company, if not the originator, was surely the popularizer of solid-colored earthenwares for the table in mix-and-match combinations; that the company had had a long, productive, and successful history in Paducah, Kentucky, before moving to Los Angeles, where it achieved even greater fame and fortune; that its offerings were an assortment of hand-thrown, molded, and slip-cast wares; that no matter how extensive its lines of tablewares, kitchenwares, florist artwares, and utilitarian products for farm and family, its common red-clay flower pots, now almost wholly forgotten, were always its mainstay; that while most pieces are marked, many are not, and that is why an ever-increasing number of collectors make fascinating discoveries almost every day; and that, sadly, when the company closed, it closed for good, they would have hit the mark.

My own introduction to Bauer pottery took place in May 1976 in the Central California coastal town of Arroyo Grande. A friend, Wendell Perry, an antiques collector and collectibles dealer of voracious appetite and near-manic gusto, was desperately eager, as always, to share his latest discovery. Dropping to his knees, he began pulling mixing bowls, entire nesting sets, from kitchen cabinets, surrounding himself on the floor. I remember it as a sort of performance, a ballet of dancing bowls with Wendell's breathless narration. Those bowls spoke to the fundamental aesthetic of my soul: a form repeated over and over again in ever-changing colors. These colors were particularly appealing: apple green, honey brown, rose pink, sky blue, and sunny yellow in bowls with wide, concentric bands; jade green, red-orange, Chinese yellow, cobalt blue, and glistening black in bowls with narrow, concentric rings. And the prices, Wendell confided with equal enthusiasm, were dirt cheap.

That would have been about right for a novice freelance writer. Checking back in notebooks I began keeping soon afterward, I see that I first paid 75¢ to $1.25 apiece for bread and butter plates and saucers. I paid $8.75 for five nine-and-a-half-inch dinner plates: two yellow, one ivory, one green, one delph blue; $1.50 for a white; $2.50

apiece for two pale burgundies. I paid $1.00, $2.50, $2.65, $3.00 for bowls of various dimensions. I went out on a limb—$5.00—for a small black serving bowl and suffered a veritable *crise de conscience* over $6.00 for a pink "Aladdin's lamp" teapot in mint condition. $6.00! Was there no limit to this sybaritic indulgence? But then soon afterward I got myself in check and bought a round, covered ringware butter dish, orange, for just $3.75 at a half-price sale. In Salt Lake City I acquired four ring tumblers with wood and copper handles for $8.00. A short time later at the Rose Bowl Flea Market in Pasadena, teardrop-shaped coffee carafes were bringing up to $3.50. Ultimately, I bought Wendell's collection: 250 pieces for $200. I don't know whether to laugh now or cry.

Need it be said that values have escalated, that the price of several hundred pieces of Bauer pottery back in the Dark Ages can easily be expended on a single item today? What would J. Andy Bauer say if he knew that a simple, brown, slip-glazed merchandise crock brings $175; a hand-decorated yellowware jug and two matching mugs, $350; a black-glazed ringware cookie jar, $1,800; a ringware pitcher and six beer steins, $2,200; a statuesque, hand-thrown carnation jar, $2,500; or a pair of cobalt oil jars, $3,500? Take heart. Bargains do continue to appear, and frankly more interesting items are constantly being offered. Collectors may in foolish desperation—or from other motivations—pay large prices for lovely, but essentially commonplace objects, while genuinely rare items, harder perhaps to identify, seldom fetch top dollar.

The more you know about the things you admire—their derivation, their history, their aesthetic distinction and technical composition—the more you will appreciate and cherish them. Hence this book.

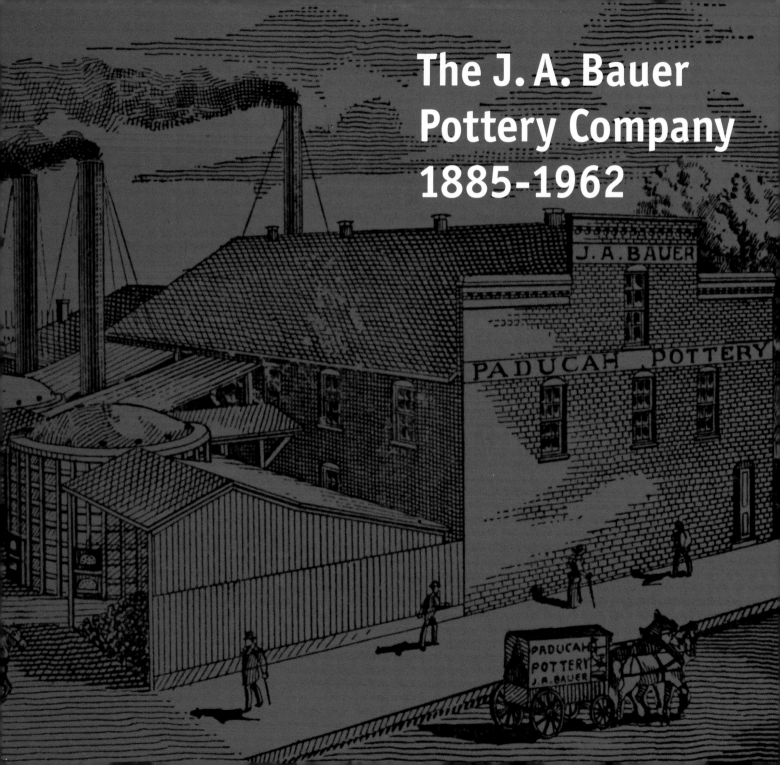

The J. A. Bauer Pottery Company 1885-1962

Iven somewhat to obsequity in the manner of *Who's Who, The Memorial Record of Western Kentucky* (1904) described J. Andy Bauer as "a genial, public-spirited man, and one who makes and retains friends. He is well and favorably known throughout a wide territory, and the success which has attended his efforts is well merited." Forty-eight years old, Bauer had by then served six years on the Paducah, Kentucky, school board, was a Democrat, a member of the Odd Fellows, and a Mason. He had married Emma Dargel of Louisville in 1884. Five of their eight children survived infancy.[1]

The following year, 1905, in a report prepared by the Kentucky Geological Survey, the characterization of Bauer's enterprise was hardly less enthusiastic: "The most important pottery of the Purchase [an area of western Kentucky obtained by the federal government from the Chickasaw in 1818] considering the extent of the factory and the modern methods of manufacture, is the Paducah Pottery, operated by Mr. J. A. Bauer."[2]

Bauer was the right person in the right place at the right time. His acumen was prodigious; the era and location, propitious. He established his pottery in a day when tariffs on imports were particularly high, favoring domestic wares. He located his operation at the confluence of rail and river transport, while competitors in the East still depended on the sea. He discovered and developed local resources, while others were importing theirs. He attended to the

Miniature presentation jugs, Paducah Pottery

capital improvement of his property, turning out a modern and diversified line of goods, supplying regional industries—vinegar, cider, whiskey, and patent medicines—with the finished clay goods they needed and other potters with the raw materials they required. What is more, he invested wisely—and not solely in pottery. By the time he left Kentucky for California in 1909, he was, in the words of Mrs. James Bauer, daughter-in-law of his youngest brother, George, "a prominent local millionaire."[3] Well, almost.

Bauer is a common German noun, meaning "farmer" or "peasant." Perhaps it occurs so frequently as a surname in America because the officials at ports of entry were not fastidious in recording the oddly spelled and unpronounceable names of the millions of immigrants who streamed into this country, almost six million of them from Germany alone between 1820 and 1930. Andreas Bauer, twenty-five, and his wife, Julianna Schlosser Bauer, twenty-four, emigrated from Bavaria in 1851. In Europe they had been *bauern*, farmers. In Jeffersonville, Indiana, where they settled, Andreas worked at the "pork house" and later as a bricklayer or plasterer. The area, like many of the states along the Ohio and Mississippi Rivers, had a substantial German population. Andreas himself was a founder in 1860 of St. Luke's German Reform Church in Jeffersonville.[4] For thirty years no English was permitted there.[5]

The Bauers had seven children: their first, Johann (later John) was born in 1852; their third, Andreas (later J. Andy), four years later. Andy attended public schools and like many of his contemporaries, began his career at the Howard Ship Yard and Dock Company,[6] the largest inland builder of steamboats in the United States. Jeffersonville produced rail cars, beer, and glass as well.[7] There were also numerous potteries; during Andy Bauer's boyhood, no less than a dozen in Jeffersonville and nearby towns of Clark County; several were operated by families with names like Bruner,

Andreas Bauer family record from archives, St. Luke's German Reform Church (now United Church of Christ), Jeffersonville, Indiana

Dietz, Hochadel, Unser, and Welker, all first-generation Americans from Germany.[8]

Until the beginning of the nineteenth century potting on the wheel was largely a part-time occupation in America, something to see a farmer through the winter months. Clays were locally dug, and wares were locally sold. Brown slip-glazed and salt-glazed stonewares, most were unadorned utilitarian forms. Tableware of any finesse was almost entirely imported, primarily from England. "Modern" mold-made forms accompanied industrialization later in the century with workshops and factories growing up where

materials, fuel for kilns, and transport were located. In 1875 forty-one such substantial potteries, concentrated in Ohio and New Jersey, formed the United States Pottery Association to stimulate consumption of domestic product, promote tariffs, foster development of the industry, and forestall incipient unionization.[9]

Andy Bauer's eldest brother, John, established his Preston Street Pottery in Louisville just across the river from Jeffersonville in about 1878. There, without much mechanization, he manufactured jugs and miscellaneous stonewares. The output was consumed locally, though distribution broadened gradually. In 1878 Andy left the shipyard and joined his brother, working initially, along with brother Christian Bauer (b. 1854), as a teamster and remaining six years. (John died of cerebral apoplexy in May 1901. The company was renamed the John Bauer Pottery Works in 1903 by his widow. As late as 1905 it was supplying glaze ingredients—Albany-type slip, red lead, and manganese—to other potteries. Mrs. John Bauer was its proprietor until 1906. A new owner, S. O. Snyder, renamed it the Louisville Pottery Company and moved it to 731 Brent Street. It was sold and renamed the Louisville Stoneware Company in 1971 and continues operating to this day.)[10]

In 1885 twenty-nine-year-old J. Andy Bauer bought out Frank Parham's Paducah Pottery[11] at 618-622 Seventh Street, corner of Trimble Avenue, and moved west with his bride. The family lived across the street at 621. In the Paducah city directory of 1890-91 Bauer's is the only pottery listed.

Miniature presentation jug, John Bauer Pottery Works

Brown slip-glazed and Bristol-glazed stonewares, Paducah Pottery

Cobalt-stenciled whiskey jugs, Paducah Pottery

Located near the confluence of the Cumberland, Ohio, and Tennessee Rivers and fifty miles from the confluence of the Ohio and Mississippi and served by the Central Illinois and St. Louis & Paducah railroads, Paducah was—and would remain—a prominent point of transit for products to and from the South and East. Occupied early in the Civil War by the Union Army, whose fort was located where Trimble (now called Martin Luther King) met the Ohio River, the city had witnessed a single skirmish (in which troops led by the Confederate general Nathan Bedford Forrest unsuccessfully attacked the Union garrison on March 25, 1864) and was spared the destruction the war wrought on other communities.

The pottery's early years saw a diversified line of unornamented, brown-glazed, hand-thrown wares—merchandise crocks; pickling jars; jugs for cider, vinegar, and whiskey; churns; and shallow pans—some debossed with the company mark, others with the names of manufacturers, distillers, and distributors scratched into the glaze, often in a distinctive, back-slanting script. These inscriptions give evidence of widespread distribution throughout Kentucky, Tennessee, Mississippi, and Texas. The line was broadened by the turn of the century to include growlers (containers for beer bought by the measure), mugs, cuspidors, filters, measures, coolers, jars, nappies (shallow serving dishes), bail-handled jugs, druggists' jugs, flue thimbles, and vases. With the advent of the "sanitary revolution," when white wares were thought to be inherently more healthful than the often unattractive slip-glazed browns, the line came to include Bristol-glazed jugs, milk pans, butter and bean pots, pie plates, mixing bowls, water coolers and filters, lovely blue mottled (cobalt spongeware) dresser sets (basins and ewers), slop jars and chamber pots, chicken founts and pigeon nests, and pitchers plain or with grapes in molded relief (almost identical to ones manufactured in neighboring Evansville, Indiana, by Uhl). There

Engraved view of the Paducah Pottery, from Kentucky of To-Day, *1896*

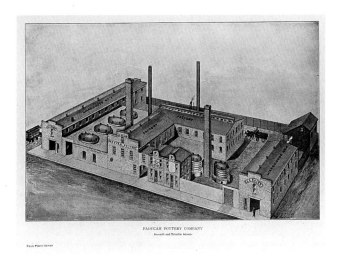

Engraved view of the Paducah Pottery, from "Paducah" The City Beautiful, *c. 1903–8*

were also redwares for the garden: flower pots and saucers; seed, bulb, and fern pans; elaborate lawn vases of vaguely classical design; and hanging baskets.[12] The brown-glazed and inscribed jugs gave way to white or white-and-brown jugs marked with cobalt stencils. A sales brochure of the period reads, "Paducah Pottery Company / Sanitary Stoneware, Stoneware Specialties / and Red Flower Pots / The Largest Factory in the South."

Indeed the Paducah Pottery was large and despite the muddled account in Paul Evan's oft-cited standard, *Art Pottery of the United States*, prosperous. Engraved views indicate significant growth over the years. The earlier view (1896) shows at least four kilns, three stacks, a factory building, and sheds. Sixty men were at that time employed. The later view (c. 1903-8) shows the addition of at least two kilns and a stack, a factory building, two warehouses, offices, a shed, and other structures along Trimble Avenue.

The 1905 geological report goes on to say, "The clays…are gotten from various points. A considerable quantity is obtained from Mr. Bauer's mines at Boaz [pronounced 'bows'], in Graves county,"[13] fourteen miles south on the Illinois Central Railroad. Those directions were published when steam locomotive and donkey cart were the conveyances of the day, yet the site remains remarkably easy to find. The cart that was used to dump refuse along the banks of the Ohio River may have circled around to Boaz to carry clay back to town. One can find Bristol-glazed shards in the clay pit to this day.

"The bed is composed of three feet of a creamy-white clay, underlaid by two feet of a stiff purple clay, both containing impressions of fossil leaves," the state geologist reported. "Little trouble is experienced in getting out clay for shipment or local use, as the surface covering is but a few feet thick until the bluffs are reached some distance eastward."[14] In addition to the Boaz clay, Bauer is reported to have used clay from the property of Victor Welch "on the Lone Oak and Mayfield Road, four miles southwest of Paducah," still identifiable on city maps.

The report intimates one key to Bauer's success: while others were still importing their clays from England or at best shipping them upriver from Missouri and Tennessee, Bauer was actively sampling the local resources, providing himself—and his customers—with cheap, reliable materials. The esteemed Rookwood Pottery in Cincinnati, Ohio, analyzed and tested numerous samples of Purchase clays, some collected on behalf of the Kentucky Geological Survey by Bauer himself. The resultant wares were exhibited at the Louisiana Purchase Exposition (1904), where they won a gold medal.[15] The Paducah Pottery was itself represented at the fair in the Kentucky Mineral Exhibit in the Palace of Mines and Metallurgy by a miniature pottery works, turning out molded product made from McCracken and Graves county clays.[16]

Granted that coincidence and causation are two entirely different things, Bauer's presence at the fair in St. Louis appears to have been fortuitous. Ceramic exhibits were legion at the fair; matte green Grueby-type glazes, ubiquitous.[17] Among the exhibitors was Norse Pottery,[18] whose principal designer and mold maker was a Danish-trained potter, Louis Ipsen, who would join Bauer in Los Angeles about a decade later and remain more than three decades with the firm. Another exhibitor, albeit on a grander scale, was the relentlessly self-promoting county of Los Angeles. Its fantastical display, upholstered in green velvet and outlined in seedless oranges, portrayed the county as an Eden of astonishing luxuriance, the climatological wonder of the world, whose three hundred annual days of sunshine were the fabled panacea for every ailment.[19]

Typical Los Angeles boosterism on a postcard published 1908

Anyone with an eye on the news in the early months of 1994 will be familiar, by contrast, with the intermittent savagery of winters in western Kentucky. The Bauer family, like numerous prosperous southerners and midwesterners, took to wintering in Southern California—Bauer in search of relief from asthma. Or could it have been silicosis? (Pottery tycoon Homer Laughlin moved from Ohio to Los Angeles in 1901.) By early 1909 Bauer had selected a site for a new pottery, and the following year by chartered train in the company of his wife, daughters Katie, Eva, Mayme, and Tillie, son Edwin, key employees, a pony, and several dogs, he joined the hordes that more than trebled the population of the city (from 102,000 to 319,000) in the first ten years of the century. Among the travelers were kiln bosses John Overstreet and Culley Jackson; his son, Bernard Jackson (who would still be with the company half a century later); and Watson E. Bockmon, under whose management the company ultimately authored the most colorful chapter in the history of American dinnerware.[20]

The J. A. Bauer Pottery Company was built on West Avenue 33 in Lincoln Heights, an industrial suburb midway between Los Angeles and Pasadena. Half a dozen potteries, surrounded by workers' cottages, were already located nearby. Rail lines were close at hand for the transportation of materials and wares. The building at 415-421 West Avenue 33 was ready for occupancy in 1910.

Sales flyer, c. 1909–13, Paducah Pottery

Bristol-glazed wares

Two-gallon fumigators

Identical illustrations in sales literature from Paducah (late) and Los Angeles (early) reveal that molds brought from Kentucky included those for agricultural, mercantile, industrial, and domestic items. American farm families still cooled milk in Bristol-glazed pans and churned butter by hand. Stores still stocked merchandise in crocks; Bauer's came in a score of sizes, from one-half to sixty gallon. Professional distillers demanded jugs, and in 1920, when Prohibition came into effect nationwide (some states had already been dry for years), amateurs demanded ceramic jars. Rather than staining woods, furniture makers "fumed" their mission-style goods with powerful ammonia solutions in heavy, juglike fumigators. Indoor plumbing had long since become de rigueur, but some older homes undoubtedly continued to require chamber pots; and hotels and taverns, spittoons. The humble, brown-glazed cuspidor remained in the line long enough to be revivified in blue and green art pottery glazes and to serve as a model for molded floral items.

All this might signify a conservative enterprise transplanted, but nothing in Bauer's past suggested conservatism. Compelling photographic evidence indicates just how quickly the company adapted to its new environment. By 1910 the architectural style known as the

TOP *"Jap tub"*
BOTTOM *Bowen Court, Pasadena, c. 1912*

"California bungalow" had been articulated in residences both great and small. These were, in the words of architectural historian Robert Winter, based on the notion of "an idealized country place," in every way harmonious with its natural setting.[21] Among its most prominent proponents was the architectural partnership of Arthur and Alfred Heineman. Period photographs of Heineman-designed properties, both individual houses and bungalow courts, reveal their unsparing use of Bauer's molded redware "Jap tubs." So consistent was their incorporation that one might speculate that the Ernest Batchelder-trained Alfred designed and commissioned the tubs, and the company simply added them to the line. After all, early Bauer sales catalogues boasted, "We can furnish almost everything designed by our customers, as our turners are very artistic." (I presented this hypothesis to Winter; it failed to gain his endorsement.)

Rustic stump

Pages from J. A. Bauer Pottery Co.: High Grade Colored and Natural Finishes, *c. 1919*

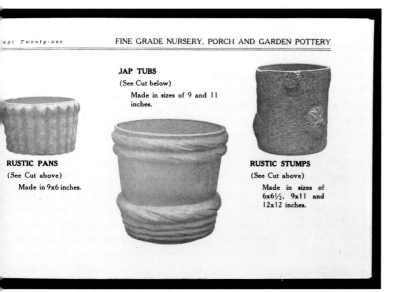

Bauer, who had manufactured redware nursery items in Paducah, expanded these offerings with plain and fancy flower pots and plant coasters in numerous shapes and sizes and added to these others consistent with the bungalow aesthetic—Indian bowls and aptly named "rustic pans" and "rustic stumps"—along with items to complement the increasing numbers of more conventional mansions on "millionaires row" in Montecito, Pasadena, Redlands, and Santa Barbara.

Who modeled these varied redwares is unknown, though one wonders if longtime Bauer stalwarts could have altered their vernacular so radically. Perhaps recruits from the numerous neighboring competitors or employees of the Los Angeles Pottery Company, a maker of red-clay pots on nearby Griffin Avenue, which Bauer bought out in his first months in Los Angeles, brought knowledge of former employers' wares.[22]

The redwares seem unlikely, however, to owe anything to Louis Ipsen, who left Rockford, Illinois, and Norse Pottery in 1907 and whose next known address was Los Angeles in 1915. It was common for Bauer employees to live within walking distance of the plant in its early years, so it is questionable that Ipsen worked for Bauer earlier than 1915 while living beyond the limits of the city. He does not appear as a Bauer employee in the city directory until 1916. He then is listed as a clay worker in 1917, potter in 1918, foreman in 1921, and factory superintendent from 1925. Nor are the redwares likely to have been the work of another, now-renowned Bauer potter, Matt Carlton, who, according to his son, Delbert, brought his family to Los Angeles in the early months of 1915 and went to work immediately as a kilnburner at Pacific Clay Products, which had only recently begun the production of stonewares. It is not known when Carlton joined Bauer. He first appears as a laborer in residence about a block from the plant in the city directory of 1917.

The dates of Ipsen's and Carlton's employment are a matter of import to collectors because of a familiar photograph showing a prize-winning J. A. Bauer Pottery Co. exhibit at the Panama-California International Exposition. The display is distinctly marked "art pottery" and prominently includes, along with Bauer redwares (the large bell vases, hanging bells and baskets, ollas, and Indian bowls), artwares invariably attributed to Ipsen and Carlton: molded floral items in the case of the former and elegant, often monumental, hand-thrown Rebekah vases and carnation jars in the case of the latter. The fair opened January 1, 1915, prior to the arrival of either man. The photo is faintly dated 1916. The wares in the exhibit, not to mention the "art pottery" sign, could have been changed any number of times during the two-year run of the fair. Then again, attributions commonly made to Ipsen and Carlton may be inaccurate. Rebekah vases and hand-thrown cylindrical forms appear in an even older photograph of a float representing Bauer Pottery in a November 1913 industrial parade.

What is undoubtedly ill-founded is the latter-day evaluation of the bronze medal—perhaps the framed citation propped against the counter in the photograph—awarded the display. This was far from the lofty "third place" one sees heralded. There were, in fact, four grand prizes (all to European manufacturers), eight gold medals (including five to Californians: Alberhill Coal and Clay Company, Ernest Batchelder, Cornelius Brauckman, Frederick H. Rhead, later the designer of Homer Laughlin's post-moderne Fiestaware, and Fred H. Robertson), six silver medals, and two bronzes (one to Bauer and one to Miss Olive Newcomb).[23] The jury published no criteria, but in context, the Bauer and Newcomb citations seem merely to have acknowledged their participation.

Panama-California International Exposition, San Diego, 1916

Molded artwares, probably designed by Louis Ipsen

Parade float, 1913. J. Andy Bauer is standing at left.

World War I concluded, industry in Los Angeles marched to a new tune:

Keep the smoke stacks smoking, every stoker stoking.
Now the boys are coming home, work can't be slack.
Start new wheels ahumming, send new drummers drumming.
Turn your pockets inside out, it will all come back.[24]

Business in 1919 was "ahumming" all over town. Bauer constructed a two-story brick addition and an office bungalow. The Industrial Week celebration the following May featured a parade four miles long. "Especially interesting," in the eyes of *The Clay-Worker*, "was the float of the J. A. Bauer Pottery Co., showing not only a good line of their products, but two potters at work, an entire vessel being moulded and shaped during the progress of the parade. They likewise had a beautiful exhibit of their art pottery in the window of Fowler Bros., leading stationers of the city." Shops throughout L.A. displayed local clay products; in addition to Bauer's, those of the Alberhill Coal and Clay Company, Italian Terra-Cotta, Los Angeles Press Brick, Pacific Clay Products, and Southern California Clay Products, among others. The city counted 2,700 industrial establishments producing $618 million in goods, a rise of 60 percent over 1918.[25]

A thirty-five page Bauer sales catalogue of the day shows that the floral artware line, though subtly redesigned and offered in a wider range of "high grade colored and natural finishes," remained largely unchanged, as did the redwares. Brown-glazed utilitarian wares had all but given way to white (though a curious Albany-type slip glaze, spiked with manganese in dramatic, lustrous drips made its appearance at this time). The variety of domestic yellowwares—pitchers, mayonnaise jars, bowls of various shapes and numerous sizes—had more than doubled. Last, but surely not least in the hearts of collectors, was the debut of a decorative new logo:

19

Cobalt-stenciled label

the cobalt-stenciled California orange with "J. A. Bauer / Pottery Co. / Los Angeles" emblazoned on its side.[26]

Bauer, a prosperous man when he moved to Los Angeles, was even more affluent a decade later. To the degree that the bungalow style could yield a mansion, he lived in one, called Four Oaks on Fair Oaks in South Pasadena, a two-story, shingle behemoth on a half city block with gardens, tennis courts, stables, and a pond. Bauer himself built houses in the bungalow style for each of his children when they married, several on a single block of Pasadena Avenue that he also owned. (He later gave each of his children rural acreage.) On Sundays he enjoyed driving the Studebaker down to his ranch in Norwalk. An active Shriner, a member of the Los Angeles Athletic Club, San Gabriel Country Club, and First Church of Christian Science, a doting grandfather, a devout Protestant—he read his Bible each morning upon rising and sang hymns in the shower—and a world traveler, in 1922, at age sixty-six, he retired. He sold a two-thirds interest in the J. A. Bauer Pottery Company for $40,000 to the family of Bernard Bernheim, a Louisville whiskey magnate looking for an investment while sitting out Prohibition, and the remaining third for $20,000 to his second eldest daughter, Eva Elizabeth, and her husband, Watson Bockmon. Thereafter, still vibrant, he spent his days in an office in downtown Los Angeles doing we know not what. Then on October 31, 1923, J. Andy Bauer died in his sleep, leaving an estate with an appraised value of $525,000. His substantial portfolio of investments included, besides Four Oaks and the ranch, a dozen other properties in Los Angeles and the mortgages on another ten.[27]

J. Andy Bauer, c. 1920

Watson E. ("Wat") Bockmon had idolized his father-in-law. He dressed like him, wore his hair like him, emulated him in every detail, converting to the Christian Science faith when Bauer did. (His first son, John Andrew Bockmon, died in childhood the year Bauer retired.) Once a traveling salesman for a Bockmon family coffee company, he had served Bauer Pottery as bookkeeper, sales representative, and superintendent.[28] Now he would be its president. Bernheim entrusted his interests to his sons: Lynn was named vice-president; Samuel, secretary-treasurer. The relationship endured uneasily for five years. Bockmon's watchword was thrift; Sam didn't know its meaning. Bockmon regretted money spent paving the muddy yard; Sam called on customers in a leather-covered, chauffeur-driven Lincoln landau (parked several blocks away lest the customer, the proprietor of a neighborhood hardware store, for instance, be given an impression of ostentation and inflated prices). In October 1929 at a cost of $4,000 the Bernheims erected a steel-framed, 3,400 square foot concrete shed with steel-plated doors and a galvanized metal roof for storage of the master molds; Bockmon shuddered at their profligacy (though the investment saved his hide a few years later).[29]

During this partnership the line could be said to have evolved rather than expanded. There was a subtle design change in the knop of the poultry fount; mugs and marmalades joined the yellowware domestic line; glaze was applied to the stoneware jardinieres; a flower holder in the form of a half orange was included among the florist items; and Louis Ipsen added new forms to his repertoire of molded artwares (these were fired to a semivitreous hardness, then glazed on the inside only). In 1926, after the discovery of Tutankhamen's tomb had been widely publicized and the romance of ancient Egypt swept the popular imagination, he modeled a commemorative vase.[30]

In 1927 the unhappy partnership broke apart. Lynn Bernheim ascended to the presidency; Sam became vice-president and treasurer. Bockmon, retaining the family stake, departed active management.

Bauer Pottery was part of a sizable clay community. In 1928 the Los Angeles clay industry employed 4,700 workers in forty-five manufacturing concerns. Of these only a handful were making stonewares, ollas, semivitreous whitewares, vitreous china, garden pottery, and specialties. The rest were supplying products for the booming construction juggernaut: brick; sewer pipe; hollow, roof, and facing tiles; and sanitary wares.

The story of the manufacture of clay products used by the building trades, beginning in Southern California in the 1880s, was one of repeated consolidations and enlargements. Two results of these mergers were Pacific Clay Products and Gladding, McBean. Southern California possessed some of the nation's largest plants.

The terra-cotta clays required for redware were common along the shore. Clays for stoneware were mined principally in Orange, Riverside, San Bernardino, and San Diego Counties. Gladding, McBean had its own clay mine near the town of Lincoln, in Placer County, north of Sacramento. Clays from several sites were often necessary for a good stoneware body, making the manufacture of stoneware costlier in California than in the East. Some clays, such as ball and china clays, were imported from England or the eastern United States, and some were brought south by Gladding, McBean and Bauer, among others, from Ione, in Amador County, east of Sacramento, as well as Lincoln.

While California was able to serve more of its own needs for clay construction products than was any other state, its sales to other regions were minimal. Red-clay construction materials were made nationwide, generally near where they were required, and delivery by rail was expensive.

"The statistics on clay products imported," a Los Angeles Chamber of Commerce study (1928) reported:

show quite clearly that the opportunities for expanding the clay products industry lies very largely in the finer wares, such as china and earthenware. ...There is no doubt that the value of clay products brought into Southern California is several times that of the products manufactured in Southern California and shipped out of state. Such wares imported include ordinary earthenware kitchenware, sanitary wares, vitreous tablewares, and art pottery.[31]

A report prepared by Waldemar Fenn Dietrich for the state division of mines and minerals gives this factual summary of the business at about the time of the split between Bockmon and the Bernheims:

[Bauer] is a four-kiln pottery making a complete line of red flower pots, white stoneware, yellow bowls, crocks, vases, and ollas. Santa Monica clay is used for flower pots and ollas, while Alberhill [Riverside County] and Lincoln clays are used for the light-colored, vitrified stoneware bodies. Approximately 4,000 tons of clay are consumed per year [Pacific Clay Products, by comparison, had capacity for 90,000 tons of clay products per year at four plants]....

Flower pots and some of the other ware are machine molded. For other products turning ("jiggering") or hand moulding are used. All of the smaller ware is dried in 24 hours, natural gas auxiliary heating being used in the drying room. White, yellow or cream glazes, where used, are applied by dipping before firing. A single firing matures both the body and the glaze.

The four kilns are of the round down-draft type, fired with gas, but equipped to burn oil if necessary or desirable. The red ware is burned to a temperature of 1850°F in three to four days, and the cream body ware is fired to 2250°F in about the same time. One of the kilns is ordinarily operating on the light-colored body, and is equipped with pyrometric control.

At present this is the only plant in Los Angeles manufacturing flower pots. Not over half the company's business is in flower pots, but this constitutes the largest single item. In order to permit the full-time operation of the plant on a systematized plan, a stock of ware aggregating over $100,000 in value is constantly kept on hand.

Fifty men are employed.[32]

Plant One, 1930s

The Bernheims experienced disappointing response to their offerings. Given the Bauer production method—filling orders out of a substantial inventory rather than production on demand—a considerable stock of products existed. The Bernheims recognized the need for change. One response was the hiring of a Mexican thrower of red-clay art- and gardenwares. A second was the initiation of a dinnerware line, an apparent collaboration between Ipsen and Carlton with spare, unmodulated shapes, offered in yellowware. A third, the determination to offer these wares in color, led to the hiring of a young ceramic engineer, Victor Houser.[33]

What was generally being offered to the consumer for domestic use at this time? In a word, white. Porcelain, china, and earthenware in white or ivory with decoration, if any, in gold, decalcomania, or over- and underglaze painting. Some earthenwares were artificially tinted with metal oxides and sold with transparent or semitransparent glazes as yellowware. Dinnerware was purchased in sets or as open stock, and the majority was from England. The American Ceramic Society was forced to consider from the dais and in print "Why American Pottery Is Not the Vogue in America," concluding:

As long as the American potters stand in awe of centuries of experience and reputation, just so long will the American public prefer tableware other than American-made. . . . In short, we do not try to find out what the public wants, and how much. We make what we think the dealer ought to buy and then wait for him to come down to our plants and buy it. The public is ignorant of an American product. Consequently there is no public demand.[34]

Leaves from promotional photo album, c. 1928

Yellowware dinner service

Leaf from promotional photo album, c. 1928

Some decisions can be viewed as inspiration, some as opportunism, some as inevitabilities. To what factors, apart from inspiration and the evident disproportion of imports noted by the 1928 Chamber of Commerce study, can the Bauer Pottery decision to manufacture brightly colored earthenwares be attributed? The clays for the manufacture of earthenwares were available to the Bernheims locally and inexpensively. Earthenware bodies are highly plastic; a technician with only modest skill and training can form more bodies in a given time than he can with china or porcelain. Dried earthenware is stronger; less care is required and more speed is possible in finishing and placing wares in the kiln for bisque firing. Firing is at lower temperatures, resulting in less shrinkage and warpage. Because earthenware is relatively porous, it absorbs glaze more readily. The range of temperatures at which glazes mature is greater, and acceptable wares are produced in more varied conditions, which was important at Bauer, where tablewares were at first packed in kilns with redwares and stonewares. Kilns can be packed more efficiently with earthenwares, resulting in lower labor costs; and fuel costs are lower than with china or porcelain. Given earthenware's greater tolerances, more processes can be handled mechanically. High-lead glazes, the kind first developed, fire at lower temperatures than low-lead glazes or those with substitutes for lead.[35]

Houser recalls that when he arrived:

Bauer had made or was making a limited line of garden pottery and floral items—vases and stuff for the floral industry—and they were using a green glaze and a blue glaze and what was almost a transparent glaze, which fired to a light yellow, kind of dirty yellow. They put all of that on the stoneware body and fired it in the stoneware kilns. Of course, they had the brown glaze too, which they made from a brown clay, which you could buy on the market. That was about it.

The Bernheims were finding out the stuff was a little too crude. They wanted to improve the business and enlarge it; the Depression hadn't quite arrived yet. So they hired me to make some colored glazes, and they hired another fellow who was a terra-cotta designer and moldmaker. He modeled some terra-cotta shapes, garden pottery and stuff.

Really, I don't think they knew what they wanted for sure. They were just feeling their way. They knew they wanted to make some nicer-looking stuff that would sell. They had kind of a crummy set of mixing bowls; I think that yellow glaze was the only thing they put on that. They even had a little set of dishes. I don't know whether they ever sold any or not. Flat, very flat. And thick. And very Spanish. So, there was stuff to try my glazes on: blue, yellow, green.

One thing the Bernheims wanted was a set of flower pots, colored flower pots, that little ruffle pattern. The salesmen went for this stuff, and they started selling it. Then, of course, we started making other shapes that the trade would go for, largely dishes. Those we bisque fired and hand-dipped in a tub of glaze. Color was apparently everything then, so I worked on different colors.[36]

Glazes (RIGHT) in use at the time of Victor Houser's arrival at Bauer and the first three glazes (LEFT) he formulated there

William Wrigley's Catalina and Durlin Brayton's Laguna potteries—the former isolated, though assiduously advertised, the latter minuscule—began dabbling in solid-colored earthen tablewares at about the same time as Bauer.[37] Whether the Bernheims were familiar with them is unknown and perhaps irrelevant. Bauer gets the credit for first penetrating the market with a line of brightly colored earthenwares and demonstrating persuasively the appropriateness of mixing colors in a place setting, let alone on the table. Together what was to become known as the "Big Five"—Bauer; Gladding, McBean; Metlox; Pacific; and Vernon—persuaded homemakers to put pottery in place of porcelain on the dining room table. "Pottery dishes, no longer crude, are equally at home during the serving of a formal meal or at a lawn fete," the boosterish *California—Magazine of Pacific Business* crowed in 1937. "So much at home, in fact, that manufacturers will turn out $2,000,000 worth of pottery dinnerware this year; ware which eight years ago was virtually unknown."[38]

Despite the almost immediate success of their colored wares, the Bernheims' fortunes were not reversed. In Houser's words:

They had a peculiar way of operating their business. They seemed to think that they could dictate to the customer. For one thing they had plant hours, and at 4:30, why, the place closed down; everybody went home. Customers sometimes would come a little bit late. Well, if the place was locked up, fine, but Jim Bockmon [Watson's nephew], who had more or less charge of the office, and I would sometimes sit out on the front steps after work and talk, and while we would be there, why, a customer would come, and he'd want to buy some crocks or something. Now, Jim was told to say, "We're closed," and the customer would say, "Well, can't you open the gate and let me in and get six crocks?" "No, the rule says we're closed, and that's that."

Selection of Catalina pottery (LEFT) *and Brayton Laguna* (RIGHT)

That was just one little example of the Bernheims' attitude. The customer had to conform, and customers don't do that. So they weren't having too much business by that time, and they were apparently doing their darnedest to chase that away. They were probably losing money.

I guess they got disgusted with the way things were going, and maybe they saw the Depression coming on, so they talked to Wat Bockmon...No, I think Bockmon probably came to them. Maybe it was kind of a mutual thing: Bockmon wanted back into pottery, and they wanted to get the heck out. See, when Bockmon left Bauer, he agreed not to go into the pottery business, so he started a little plant out east of Maywood making floor tile out of red clay. He didn't know the first thing about how to sell floor tile; that was a business in itself apparently. So one day I was working for the Bernheims, and the next day I was going to work for Wat Bockmon. He didn't do anything at the time except just take over and try to get back some of the customers that the Bernheims had driven away. I was told years later that he said that he was going to get rid of that glaze man, because he didn't want to mess around with that sort of thing. He did get rid of the guy that was making the terra-cotta shapes [hence their rarity], but somebody, I guess, talked him into keeping me.

Sam Bernheim went Hollywood: he married a starlet, burned his candle at both ends, and died young. Lynn Bernheim went native: he got into real estate, moved to Beverly Hills, and lived to a ripe, old age.[39] At Bauer Bockmon was back in command, and to celebrate, the company distributed a commemorative stoneware medallion. Beneath the legend "J. A. Bauer Pottery Co., Los Angeles, Cal. / Seasons Greetings / 1929," a mounted Indian, his lance raised in triumph, gallops past a Conestoga wagon abandoned and forlorn. Read into that what you will.

Houser's surprising revelation notwithstanding, Bockmon did "mess around" with glazed pottery. Indeed, the Bockmon era (1929-39) is remembered for this and little else. That anything from the preceding forty-four years or the following twenty-three would be as highly prized today had it not been for Bauer's California ring (or "ruffled") ware is debatable. Recognition of the company almost invariably begins right here with bread and butters, butter chips, salad plates, dinner plates, chop plates, saucers, and platters; coffee cups, custard cups, eggcups, teacups, jumbo cups, goblets, tumblers, mugs, demitasse sets, and beer steins; cereal bowls, salad bowls, soup bowls, and nappies; fruit dishes, berry dishes, butter dishes oblong and round, vegetable servers oval and divided, sugar bowls and creamers capacious and diminutive, ramekins with covers and without, carafes and coffee pots ovoid and round with clay stoppers or copper lids, with handles of wood or raffia; casseroles and pedestal bowls; pitchers and punch bowls, gravy boats, decanters, ice buckets, relish dishes, teapots, salt and pepper shakers, sherbets, and sugar casters; batter bowls, beater bowls, mixing bowls in six-piece nesting ensembles; cookie jars, honey jars, mustard jars, spice jars, and refrigerator jars sold separately and in sets; cigarette jars, ashtrays, and candleholders—more than a hundred items counting variations in size and style, and all with rings, rings, lovely rings, uniform rings, rings that activate surfaces, rings that take the "earthen" out of earthenware, imparting an impression of delicacy, rings that evoke speed and breathless pleasure, rings that resemble coils, the primordial ceramic building block, rings that scatter light in colors fresh as spring, colors that engender merriment, high-gloss, high-lead, high-style colors that supplanted the translucency of porcelain at pennies per place setting in a day when every cent mattered.

Ipsen, who had designed that first "little set of dishes," designed the ring pattern as well. The round items—plates, bowls, cups (apart from their cast and applied handles)—were jiggered (a semi-automatic process requiring a revolving mold and a template). Other shapes were slip cast (with liquid clay poured into a mold, dried, and removed for firing).

Commemorative medallion, 1929

Ringware butter dishes

As Houser recalls:

The way that type of merchandise is made, they might have molds to make a hundred sets of dishes a day or so many mixing bowls a day or so many florist items, and that went on day in and day out, and if business was a little slow, Bockmon would say, "We'll make it now and stack it up, and when they want it, we'll have it." And that's the way it went. You had to have molds for your various items, and you could only make a certain amount a day. There were enough different things that you could go ahead and do that.

"Enough different things" and more added constantly, generally in response to suggestions made by wholesale customers. The ring butter dishes are a case in point. John Herbert ("Herb") Brutsche, a salesman whose territory in 1935 covered California from East Los Angeles south to the Mexican border, was handed an oblong "Depression glass" butter dish by the Parmelee-Dohrmann housewares buyer in San Diego: "We get a lot of calls for these," the buyer said, suggesting the item be copied and manufactured in clay.

Brutsche recalls:

This was the first suggestion I ever made for an item. I'd only been on the road maybe a couple of months by then. I showed it to the boss and said, "They think we could sell these." So, he had a powwow with Ipsen, and they said, "We don't want to take any chances. If we have to make a mold, and it has to be cast, it costs more. So we'll make a round one that can be jiggered." Immediately the round one sold like crazy. So they said, "Well, all right, let's add the other one." So they finally broke down and made the cast one too.[40]

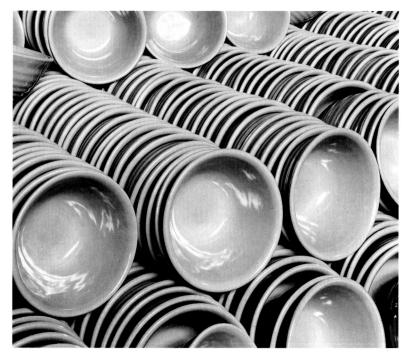

Hi-Fire bowls

While the demand for earthenware was expanding, the stoneware business was contracting. When Prohibition ended in 1933, the market for crocks fizzled. Farm wares declined as well. Demand was so low for oversize, Bristol-glazed storage jars that anything over ten gallons was simply subcontracted to the Red Wing potteries in Minnesota and stenciled with the Bauer logo. "It wasn't very long," Houser recalls, "till the colored pottery was it."

As in years past Bauer maintained an inventory and filled orders from stock. Salesmen like Brutsche made the rounds of housewares departments, hardware stores, and pottery shops. Substantial customers, jobbers like Parmelee-Dohrmann Hotel Supply, were capable of moving five hundred coffee servers in a week. A truck laden with pottery was dispatched to their warehouse daily; another, to the housewares department at Bullock's in downtown L.A. Smaller customers drove their trucks directly into the yard and loaded up a month's supply of items.[41]

"Mr. Bockmon once told me," Houser recounted, "that he'd rather have a hundred small customers than two or three big ones. That was a way to maintain a more even flow of business. If someone like Sears approached him and said, 'We'd like you to make a line for us,' he'd say no. 'If a big customer like that went belly up,' he told me, 'why, then where would you be?'"

In 1933 Bockmon commenced construction of a new beehive kiln, but even before it was finished, he started another. In 1935 he negotiated the purchase of the Batchelder-Wilson plant. The firm of Ernest Batchelder and Lucian Wilson had produced decorative architectural tiles and other ceramic products across the street from Bauer for sixteen years but had fallen victim to the Depression. Bockmon bought the property for $88,000 and immediately sold off $40,000 worth of tile left inside and three acres of the site to the city of Los Angeles for a storage yard.[42] The factory was known thereafter as Bauer's Plant Two. It was substantially different from Plant One, particularly in its use of conveyors and tunnel, or pusher, kilns. The beehive kilns at Plant One were periodic kilns, up to thirty feet in diameter, run by a crew on a rotating basis. Designed for redware and stoneware, it took several days for each kiln to achieve a maturing temperature and several more to cool down for unloading. The tunnel kilns were more appropriate for glazed wares, but instead of operating on a rotating, or periodic, basis, they had to be loaded and fired around the clock, seven days a week. Rather than being stacked and stationary, pottery traveled on fireproof cars eight to ten hours through the constantly heated kiln, pushed along by an electric motor and a giant screw.[43]

Hand-thrown Fred Johnson floral items

Display at a Los Angeles trade show, c. 1941; ringware, Monterey, and Cal-Art are prominently displayed along with objects hand-thrown by Matt Carlton and Fred Johnson

Monterey sugar and creamer set

Before Plant Two could be put into operation, however, a catastrophe occurred: a fire crippled Plant One. Typically molds for redwares were sprayed with kerosene to prevent the clay from sticking. Then the molded, but unfired wares were dried on redwood shelves over open flames before being placed inside the kiln. The almost inevitable disaster came in September 1935, just three months before the Christmas season, but because of the concrete storage building that the Bernheims had fostered over Bockmon's objections, the master molds were spared. Every worker in the plant was switched over to making plaster molds from the masters, and within thirty days production resumed at the normal pace. Brutsche, formerly a hand in the glazing department and then an in-house salesman, had become a traveling sales representative (and Bockmon's son-in-law) shortly before the fire. As he recalls, his father-in-law made $50,000 on the insurance claim.

When Plant Two went into operation several months later, the dinnerware produced there was based on a new body—talc instead of clay—formulated by Houser, who had been made superintendent. It also had a new Ipsen design, decorated with rings and bright colors like the earlier ware and marketed under the name Monterey. Also produced at Plant Two was a Hi-Fire line of kitchen, nursery, and florist items, the latter based in no small part on Niloak designs brought to Bauer by Fred Johnson, a turner who left the Benton, Arkansas, pottery for Los Angeles around 1935-36.[44]

New lines continued to be added. Ray Murray, a talented young designer who had studied art at the University of Oklahoma, came to Bauer in December 1937. Ipsen taught him to model in plaster and make molds. He set to work adding service pieces to the Monterey line—the oblong platters, the sugar and creamer set, the gravy boat, and other items—then in 1938 he began designing the Cal-Art line of inexpensive, slip cast florist items.

Also about 1938, just before Russel Wright's American Modern dinnerware line was first marketed, Murray designed the cast items for the unadorned La Linda tableware line (which shares its broad, flat rims and graceful hollow forms with Ipsen and Carlton's earlier plainware) and later the complementary Gloss Pastel kitchenware line. The familiar apple green, two-quart Gloss Pastel mixing bowl and "Aladdin's lamp" teapots are today among the most widely recognized Bauer items.[45] Ipsen contributed his design for the delicate, but short-lived El Chico line in 1938-39 as well.

For all this activity and innovation, Bauer remained a fairly modest operation, never exceeding two hundred employees, never investing substantially in automatic equipment (apart from the machines that in 1937 were producing 20,000 flower pots daily, whacking chubs of sticky red clay from long, sausagelike cylinders and stamping them into common pots of every serviceable size and dimension).[46] Yet, as Brutsche recalls, "During the Depression Bauer was the biggest money-maker in the business outside of Scio [a manufacturer of vitrified restaurant china] and Mt. Clemens [a subsidiary of the Kresge chain of five-and-dimes]. I don't think even Lenox, as old as they were, were making any money. Boy, they were all hurting, especially Homer Laughlin."

Gloss Pastel mixing bowls

Selected Bauer kitchenwares in Sears, Roebuck mail order catalogue, 1948

Sole Paducah Pottery kiln remaining after the flood of 1937

Since the J. A. Bauer Pottery Company was a sole proprietorship, not a corporation, the rewards for the stunning popularity of its product redounded solely to the benefit of the Bockmons.[47] In 1937 Watson and Eva Bockmon left the bungalow built for them by her father for a new home on the rim of a bluff with a commanding view of the Rose Bowl in Pasadena.

According to Brutsche:

Every woman in Southern California knew Bauer pottery. I was down there at Sears, Roebuck, their main buying office, in L.A. every Friday. Oh, they did a good job. They'd have a whole side of the main store with our wares. A customer couldn't miss it. Of course, we were covering eleven Western states, and we actually sold a couple of New York stores — we sold Macy's at least once — though there hadn't been much desire for the East Coast.

We were the cheapest in the business, but we didn't have the control over our customers like Gladding, McBean. They insisted that their customers had to take a 100 percent markup. In other words, if a store bought something from Gladding, McBean for fifty cents, they were bound to sell it for a dollar. Our customer would sell for eighty-nine cents.

Furthermore, Gladding, McBean was very exclusive. Usually in a town of, say, ten or twenty thousand there would be one outlet only; they'd have the line exclusively. I think that was true of Homer Laughlin too. By maintaining that policy, they had some pretty satisfied customers, even though the volume might not be the greatest.

We tried to hold it down; we would turn down certain requests. Proprietors would come into the office with a big sales pitch that they were going to outsell everybody in the business. Of course, we got some objections from the big stores once in a while, but we'd say to them, "Oh, they don't bother you." You'd give them some smooth talk. "Look, their order's nothing. The amount they sell in a month, you probably sell in two days."

In 1936 the Homer Laughlin China Company began producing Fiesta, a competitive (some would say derivative) line of talc-based, brightly glazed tablewares, at its Newell, West Virginia, plant. Admittedly Bauer's sales had been concentrated in the West, with sporadic forays into Eastern markets, but the introduction of Fiesta, made on automatic and semiautomatic equipment in enormous quantities and sold through Homer Laughlin's established sales network, effectively forestalled Bauer's widespread penetration of new markets. Still, Bockmon was not without a plan.

The Bockmon family hailed from Cookeville, Tennessee. Two brothers still lived there, and the family owned several farms. Bockmon visited at least once a year, though his wife, Eva, herself a Southerner, was unenthusiastic about the journey. A plant in the South, either Montgomery, Alabama, or Atlanta, Georgia, would give Bockmon a compelling reason to visit more often as well as providing wares closer to the large Eastern market. Atlanta, as a hub of rail transportation, got the nod, and Bockmon purchased the abandoned Virginia Dare Winery on a five-acre plot for a song.[48]

Ceramist Louis Minton designed and built the kiln there. A crew from Los Angeles followed: Bernard Jackson, who was to oversee the commencement of operations; Bob Manker, who was to run the office; and Victor Houser, who was to formulate the clay body and glazes. Houser recalls:

They wanted to find a stoneware type clay or a good talc body; they didn't know just which. So we were looking around, and in our travels, of course, we went up into Tennessee and Kentucky. Jackson, being a native of Paducah, was interested in going back and looking the place over. Why the dickens we never investigated that clay mine [in Boaz], I don't know. So we never saw the clay pits at all, but we did see the old Paducah Pottery, and, cripes, all I can remember seeing was just a few beehive kilns sitting there and practically nothing around them.

Atlanta artwares

After the close of the Paducah Pottery,[49] the factory had been converted to the manufacture of tile by F. O. Pence in the 1920s, but the catastrophic flooding of the Ohio River in 1937, the second this century, had inundated the city a good twenty blocks beyond the plant and destroyed the business forever. (A Sanford Insurance map shows that even the ruined kilns and stacks had been dismantled by the early 1940s. An auto parts store occupies much of the site today.)

Despite Bockmon's plan to compete with the large, automated potteries of the Midwest, thrift, the hobgoblin of the 1920s, got the better of him once again. Antiquated equipment—some of it out of service at Bauer for years, some of it purchased at auction—was shipped east.[50] Production of items similar but not identical to the Monterey and Cal-Art lines began early in 1939, but four months later Watson Bockmon, age fifty-four, collapsed at Santa Anita and ten days later died.

Jim Bockmon became general manager of the Los Angeles operation on behalf of his widowed aunt; Herb Brutsche took over in Atlanta. The southern branch had been incorporated as the Bauer Pottery Company—no J. A.—with ownership divided between the Bockmons and their daughter, Virginia Emma Bockmon Brutsche. Throughout 1940 it made progress toward its goal.

Brutsche remembers:

We were still bucking the big boys up Ohio way and through the East, but I had the vice-president of Sears, Roebuck down to pick our line, and I had New York salesmen who were selling some of the big floral wholesalers up there. We sold Gimbels too.

We didn't really concentrate on the dinnerware. It was the gardenware and the accessory items: the teapots, the casseroles. The casseroles were a good number in all the housewares departments.

By mid-1941 American industry saw war as inevitable. Brutsche, like others, bid on defense contracts.

Ringware pitcher with inconsistent green glaze

Our ware certainly wasn't necessary to the war effort, and I could see that all our colors would have had to be reformulated, because they had lead in them. They had copper, and copper, of course, was essential for making wire. Do you realize how much wire goes into an airplane? I knew that tin was going to be eliminated, and we were using tin oxide as an opacifier. That's what gives you the depth. You notice in some of the things that Bauer made in Los Angeles during the war the colors were thin, and that was because they were still trying to get their new opacifiers working properly. Oh, yes, some of these ceramic engineers were working overtime.

From September 1941 until just before war's end Bauer Atlanta, dedicated to war production, made nothing but two simple items under contract from the Navy: a five-inch vitrified china cereal bowl and a five-and-a-half-inch tumbler. "You could get them any color," Brutsche says, "as long as they were white." Despite these contracts, the company was constantly losing skilled employees to the military. Bauer Los Angeles, meanwhile, was not. Bockmon took no government work but avoided losing employees by reinstituting a minimal production of stoneware poultry items; the poultry industry, shipping vast amounts of chicken to the armed forces, had been declared essential to the war effort.[51]

Cereal bowl and mug, commissioned by the U.S. Navy

The standard Bauer product had failed to turn a profit for the Atlanta plant. Probate records indicate that the Bockmon estate had advanced the Georgia corporation almost $40,000 before the war. Looking ahead to the postwar years, Brutsche, now its president, determined that the corporation's future lay in sanitary wares. "My first love, my first dream, even before Pearl Harbor, was the sanitary business, because it was an open door down there; nobody in the business. And after the war we had Florida growing like crazy. These big developers were building homes around every southern state. Atlanta became a metropolis. You have no idea what the change was from prewar to postwar."

The problem was that toilets are sold fitted, and the copper, brass, and rubber needed for the fittings were classified as strategic materials. Those who had consumed these items before the war had the inside track afterward. As luck would have it, Peerless, a manufacturer of sanitary items, lost its Indiana plant to fire in 1946, and suddenly Brutsche had a willing partner with a prior claim on materials but no manufacturing facility of its own. Brutsche brought one hundred Peerless workers to Atlanta and under the trade name of Georgia Sanitary began manufacturing the Dixie line of toilets (admittedly a sidelight to the history of Bauer pottery, but for the collector who strives for absolute completeness an essential acquisition). Brutsche remained a partner until 1963; production at Georgia Sanitary continued until the late 1970s.[52]

While Bauer Atlanta never returned to the company's signature tableware and floral lines, it did experience a brief, innovative, but sadly unsuccessful flirtation with a stylish line of artwares designed by Russel Wright.

In 1938 workers at Vernon Potteries near South Central Los Angeles went on strike for higher wages. Their loyalties were divided among the AFL-affiliated International Brotherhood of Operative Potters (IBOP), the CIO, and a company union. Ultimately the IBOP prevailed, organizing the Vernon work force as well as that of Wallace China in neighboring Huntington Park.[53] In the virulently open shop atmosphere of Los Angeles, these were events that could hardly have escaped the notice of pottery owners and managers. Indeed, Brutsche recalls his father-in-law asking, "'What do you hear around about a union?' This was '37 or '38. I said, 'I haven't heard much. I don't think it's very serious.' He said, 'Well, if they organize, I'm through. I'm selling.'"

"Over my dead body!" would have been more apt. The IBOP organized Bauer workers as Local 186 in 1941.[54] Bockmon had imported workers from Cookeville, Tennessee, thinking they would stand by him in such matters.[55] Instead they were among the union stalwarts once he was gone. The local elected Carl Bockmon, a nephew, as its first defense fund collector. Fred Johnson's son, Jimmy, was elected recording secretary.[56]

In one nine-month period before the war—July 1940-April 1941—Bauer revenues from the sale of pottery in Los Angeles came to $500,000 with accounts receivable of another $73,000. The monthly payroll totaled $24,000 for two hundred employees (about seventy cents an hour on average), or roughly half of gross income.[57] In 1942 the union negotiated a 6 percent raise.[58]

The 1940s were not bad years for Bauer. Popular lines like the ringware (despite the government's embargo of certain glaze constituents), La Linda in new high-gloss colors with diminished lead and new, nonstrategic opacifiers, Gloss Pastel and Hi-Fire kitchenware, and Hi-Fire and Cal-Art florist items sold well, especially with imports from Europe and Japan blocked by the war. The early plain dinnerware, El Chico, and Monterey were phased out early in the decade. Fred Johnson appears to have left by 1940. Ray Murray left in 1941. Louis Ipsen died in 1946, and Matt Carlton, already in his mid-seventies, retired at about the same time. Of the old-timers, Houser, the glaze chemist, and Tracy Irwin, the designer who had continued developing the Cal-Art line, remained.

Employees at Plant One (OPPOSITE) and Plant Two (ABOVE), March 1938. Watson Bockmon, in suit and vest, stands smiling amidst Plant Two employees, with Herb Brutsche to his left.

Bauer was a company that responded well to the challenges of the present. But the challenges of the future? That was another story. When Brutsche returned to Los Angeles, the operations at Georgia Sanitary under way, it was 1947, and the country was in the depths of a postwar recession. Sales of Bauer pottery—like sales of everything—were dwindling.

Brutsche recalls:

People were looking for something different, especially after being exposed to Wright's American Modern, which was the most popular ware in the United States. One day we had a little meeting at Bauer: Jim Bockmon, the auditor, and I. I made the statement, "Times have changed. We've got to make a new line. If we don't, we're going to be left behind."

"Oh," the auditor speaks up, "you know, we've sold this line for umpteen years." In fact, it was now in about its fourteenth year. What did he know about the ceramic industry? What did he know about the trade? I had seen about every doggone line made in the United States. I'd been in their plants. As the attorney that we had for Watson Bockmon's probate had said, "Herb's going to get a million-dollar education back there [in Georgia]." And he was so right.

While remaining president of Bauer Pottery in Atlanta and vice-president of J. A. Bauer Pottery in Los Angeles, Brutsche, like his father-in-law a generation earlier, decamped in 1948, forming Brutsche Ceramics, first at a location in Whittier, then moving in mid-1950 to Glendale. Irwin, moonlighting, modeled the first items for the Al Fresco dinnerware line based on sketches by Brutsche. Houser formulated the glazes. The aesthetic was partly Wright (both Russel and Mary) and wholly consistent with the pronunciations of the influential design department of the Museum of Modern Art. *What Is Modern Design?* Edgar Kaufmann asked in the title of an exhibition he organized about that time, and among the precepts he published in its catalogue he included:

- Modern design should express the purpose of an object, never making it seem to be what it is not.
- Modern design should express the qualities and beauties of the materials used, never making the materials seem to be what they are not.
- Modern design should express the methods used to make an object, not disguising mass production as handicraft or simulating a technique not used.
- Modern design should blend the expression of utility, materials and process into a visually satisfactory whole.[59]

Kaufmann's precepts captured the aspiration, if not necessarily the reality, of Al Fresco. Bockmon had failed to modernize Bauer. The manufacturing process remained antediluvian: largely handwork, semiautomatic at best. Brutsche had visions of a fully automated factory, and the simple, coupe-shaped profile of Al Fresco was precisely suited to machine-made wares. The colors were, as he put it, "the colors of the day. Decorators were using those colors. Chartreuse was very, very big." His dark green was derived from a color Mary Wright had intended to use on her 1946 Country Gardens dinnerware had it gone into production as she had hoped in Atlanta.[60] In 1950, when Kaufmann organized an exhibition of home furnishings, called *Good Design*, for the Merchandise Mart in Chicago, Al Fresco was among the items displayed.[61]

Three greens: Mary Wright's Country Gardens (LEFT), *Brutsche's Al Fresco* (CENTER), *Bauer's Monterey Moderne* (RIGHT)

In no time Bockmon got the message, and despite Eva Bockmon's admonition, "I don't want you copying what Herb has done,"[62] he put into production a competing line called Monterey Moderne with similar but not identical shapes by Irwin and similar but not identical glazes by Houser. When Brutsche Ceramics folded as an independent entity (even before the exhibition in Chicago closed) and merged with Bauer, Bockmon continued both lines in the Monterey Moderne colors. While both were attractive and sold well, neither could be called wholly original in the manner of ringware. Bauer, once a leader in American tableware design, was now treading in the mainstream.

Apart from a mysterious, unnamed dinnerware line based on the intersection of a cylinder and truncated cone (the flat pieces are reminiscent of plant coasters, not unlike the very earliest Bauer dinnerware), issued in matte colors formulated by Jimmy Johnson, and a reissue of Al Fresco, now called Contempo, in the same matte colors, these were the last developments in Bauer's dinnerware history. In retrospect the years of popularity exceeded the years of innovation.

With the death of her nephew in 1955, Eva Bockmon entrusted the management of the pottery to the stalwart, aging Bernard Jackson. Revenues were so restricted that the only income realized by the corporate officers—Mrs. Eva Bockmon, her daughter, Virginia, and Virginia's husband, Herb Brutsche—were the tiny, obligatory sums granted to them as officers of the corporation. In 1960 the company lost $49,000. Whether because of this or his deteriorating eyesight, Jackson resigned (and later died of a self-inflicted gunshot wound). Brutsche rejoined the firm:

Moonsong oven-to-table accessory line

The auditor—another auditor—insisted that I come in there as general manager. I had no love for it, because our income was coming from Atlanta, outside of the $250 that I was getting a month as a director, as vice-president; it was peanuts, you know. He insisted on it. He gave me a sales talk and twisted my arm. The attorney wanted to sell the place. They wanted to get out. Everybody was feeling that way.

At the gift shows in early 1961 Brutsche introduced Contempo and a line of oven-to-table service items called Moonsong. Was its unusual profile, with handles resembling Shinto gates, a sly commentary on the overwhelming predominance of Japanese imports on the American dining room table? Perhaps. More important was its mode of manufacture. Neither jiggered nor slip cast as all previous Bauer table- and kitchenwares had been (with the exception of a handful of hand-thrown pieces), Moonsong was made on a ram press, a piece of automatic equipment that stamped each form out

of a thin slab of clay. Brutsche had succeeded at last in his goal of introducing modern technology to the factory. But to no avail. On October 2, 1961, William Rail and Bernard Rowbottom, second and tenth vice-presidents, respectively, of the IBOP, addressed Charles F. Jordan, the International's secretary-treasurer:

Dear Sir and Brother:

We are requesting Executive Board strike sanction for Local Union 186, employees of J. A. Bauer Pottery Co., Los Angeles, California.

This company is paying 20¢ per hour under the male minimum rate in dinnerware and is out to bust the union if possible.

The membership voted at a meeting on September 20, a unanimous vote of 81 in favor of striking if the contract was not settled by midnight of September 30. This is well over the required two thirds majority of the entire membership.

Fraternally yours . . . [63]

Pallets loaded with Bauer flower pots, La India Pottery Shop, Loma Linda, California, 1993

The strike was approved. The pickets went up in early October, and apart from scab labor, no further work was done. The strike continued until March 1962, when the decision was made to close the plant forever. The inventory was offered in job lots to customers who would come and take it away.[64]

Bauer had held out longer than many of its California colleagues and competitors. Haldeman went out of business in 1953; Manker, in the late 1950s. Santa Anita gave up the ghost in 1957; Vernon, in 1958. Wallace became a subsidiary of Shenango in 1959, closing entirely in 1964. By 1962 Winfield had gone bust. Eight earthenware firms outside California disappeared in 1955-58. In its Ohio and West Virginia plants Homer Laughlin was running at 50 percent of capacity in 1958, while Gladding, McBean had made arrangements for Noritake of Japan to produce American-style vitrified china with the GMB label, and Iroquois was shipping bisque dinnerware from Sango, another Japanese firm, for glazing and decorating in New York.[65]

The United States Pottery Association (USPA) sought the protection of quotas but failed to sway Congress. Writes historian Don Shotliff, "The USPA was not successful in gaining this legislative protection. Yet much of the blame rested with the lack of initiative of the employers in not revamping their operations and ware designs to create a formidable opponent for the cheaper labor nations. The few who did were able to compete on an equal basis; the rest went out of business."[66]

There is no denying that Herb Brutsche was a controversial general manager. Thirty some years later it's hard to know what this diminutive, dapper man was really like at that time. About six weeks before the strike began, he took the unusual step of addressing the staff en masse. Half an hour before quitting time everyone was asked to assemble in the paved yard between the factory and the office, and Brutsche, speaking extemporaneously, presented his view of the dire prevailing economic conditions: competition from the Japanese, the advent of plastics, the prolonged recession. "I knew they were all wondering, 'What about a raise? You didn't mention that.'" The speech violated provisions of the National Labor Relations Act; Brutsche was subpoenaed but never charged.[67]

Surviving employees almost universally blame Brutsche for Bauer's demise but fail to note that he was the one person who remained steadfast in his vision of the economic benefits of modernization. Ironically, the single Bauer asset marketable after the demise was the ram press. Maddux Pottery purchased it and for a few short months produced and marketed the Moonsong line .[68]

Notes

1. *Memorial Record of Western Kentucky*, vol. 2 (Chicago and New York: Lewis, 1904), pp. 599–600.

2. *Clays in Several Parts of Kentucky with Some Account of Sands, Marls and Limestones*, bulletin no. 6, Kentucky Geological Survey (Lexington: Office of the Survey, 1905), p. 121.

3. Mrs. James Bauer, interview with the author, 2 June 1993.

4. "In Memoriam" (obituary for Andrew [Andreas] Bauer), *Jeffersonville [Indiana] Evening News*, 14 July 1898.

5. Jeanne Burke, reference librarian, Jeffersonville [Indiana] Township Public Library, undated [approx. June 1993] letter to the author.

6. *Memorial Record*, p. 599; and payroll records of the Howard Ship Yard and Dock Company, Manuscripts Department, Lilly Library, Indiana University, Bloomington, Indiana.

7. Burke letter.

8. "Industry — Pottery and Brickyards," historical files, Jeffersonville Township Public Library. According to a bluntly titled obituary ("John Bauer, Formerly of This City, Drops Dead," *Jeffersonville [Indiana] Evening News*, 8 May 1901), John Bauer apprenticed with George Unser. It is not unlikely that Andy Bauer himself was familiar with Unser's stonewares. An early Bauer Pottery mark almost replicates Unser's customary stamp.

9. Don A. Shotliff, "The History of the Labor Movement in the American Pottery Industry: The National Brotherhood of Operative Potters-International Brotherhood of Operative Potters, 1890–1970," Ph.D. diss., Kent State University, 1977, p. 25.

10. Information in this paragraph comes from numerous sources: "The Modern Plant of the Louisville Pottery Company," *The Clay-Worker* 50 (July 1908): 23; Nettie Oliver, reference librarian, Filson Club, Louisville, Kentucky, letter to the author, 26 October 1993; Kathryn Biatcher, staff member, Filson Club, undated research notes for an article on Louisville potteries; Filson Club clipping files; Louisville city directory for 1879; *Louisville of To-Day* (Louisville: Consolidated, 1895); advertisement for Antique Researchers, *Maine Antique Digest*, August 1993.

11. *Memorial Record*, p. 599.

12. Items manufactured by the Paducah Pottery are listed in *Clays in Several Parts of Kentucky*, p. 121, and appear in a beautifully designed and printed catalogue of about 1905 and a later, undated sales circular.

13. *Clays in Several Parts of Kentucky*, p. 121.

14. Ibid., p. 110.

15. Ibid.

16. "Pottery in Operation at the Fair," *Clay Record* 23 (29 October 1903): 31.

17. "Louisiana Purchase Exposition Ceramics, Continued," *Keramic Studio* 6 (February 1905): 216–19; (March 1905): 251–52; (April 1905): 268–69; (May 1905): 7–8.

18. Sheryl J. Samuelson, "Great Danes," *Journal of the American Art Pottery Association* 9, no. 1 (January–February 1994): 9.

19. Mark Bennitt, ed., *History of the Louisiana Purchase Exposition* (St. Louis: Universal Exposition Publishing, 1905), pp. 449–50.

20. The account of the move from Paducah to Los Angeles comes from information shared in interviews with the author by Victor Houser (5 June 1993), John Herbert Brutsche (11 March 1994), and Andy Bauer's granddaughter Dorothy Hilton (21 May 1994).

21. Robert Winter, *The California Bungalow* (Los Angeles: Hennessey & Ingalls, 1980), p. 19.

22. Brutsche interview.

23. Frederick H. Rhead, untitled editorial, *The Potter* 1 (December 1916): 38.

24. "Clay Products: Brick, Tile and Pottery Manufacturers Play Conspicuous Part in Los Angeles Industrial Week Celebration in May," *The Clay-Worker* 73 (June 1920): 695.

25. Ibid., pp. 695–96.

26. *J. A. Bauer Pottery Co., Manufacturers: High Grade Colored and Natural Finishes* (Los Angeles: Bauer Pottery, c. 1919), e.g., p. 28.

27. Information in this paragraph derives from interviews with Bauer's grandchildren Dorothy Hilton, Bob Sheahan, and Dallas Speers on 21 May 1994 and subsequent telephone conversations and from Bauer's probated will on file in Los Angeles County archives.

28. Hilton interview; and city directories of Paducah (1904) and Los Angeles (various years).

29. Brutsche interview; and building permits on file in Los Angeles City archives.

30. *J. A. Bauer Pottery Co., Manufacturers: High Grade Colored and Natural Finishes* (Los Angeles: Bauer Pottery, c. 1926), p. 10.

31. "How the Clay Industry Has Grown," *Southern California Business* 7 (May 1928): 49–50.

32. Waldemar Fenn Dietrich, *The Clay Resources and the Ceramic Industry in California*, bulletin no. 99 (San Francisco: California Division of Mines and Mining, 1928), p. 98.

33. Houser interview.

34. Ross C. Purdy, "Why American Pottery Is Not the Vogue in America," *Ceramic Age* 18 (October 1931): 220, 222.

35. Arthur S. Watts, *The Selection of Dinnerware for the Home,* Engineering Experiment Station circular no. 21 (Columbus: Ohio State University, 1930), pp. 2–15.

36. This and subsequent Houser quotations are taken from interviews with the author 5 June and 3 July 1993.

37. Jack Chipman, *Collector's Encyclopedia of California Pottery* (Paducah: Collector Books, 1992), pp. 20, 24.

38. "Colored Pottery: California Manufacturers Lead the World in Beauty of Design and Coloring," *California—Magazine of Pacific Business* 27, no. 9 (September 1937): 16.

39. Brutsche interview.

40. This and subsequent Brutsche quotations are taken from interviews with the author 11 March and 1 May 1994.

41. Ibid.

42. Ibid.

43. Houser interview.

44. Arlene Hyten Rainey, interview with the author, 7 April 1994.

45. Ray Murray, interview with the author, 2 May 1994.

46. Sheahan interview.

47. Brutsche interviews.

48. Ibid.

49. The chronology with regard to the Paducah Pottery is not yet entirely clear. The pottery went right on producing its customary wares for some years after J. A. Bauer moved to Los Angeles, and Bauer remained its president (the company having been incorporated in 1905). His brother George continued his employment there. Andy Bauer's son Edwin's photo album for 1913 includes shots of the pottery taken within days of a disastrous rising of the Ohio River that year. It is possible that his father severed his ties with the pottery soon after that. At the end of the decade, however, the pottery was still operating, some of the corporate officers who had served with Bauer having stayed.

50. Brutsche interviews.

51. Ibid.

52. Ibid.

53. Shotliff, "History of the Labor Movement," p. 274.

54. Documents in box 84, folder 53, archives of the International Brotherhood of Operative Potters (IBOP), Special Collections and Archives, Kent State University Library (KSUL).

55. Houser interviews.

56. IBOP documents, KSUL.

57. Watson E. Bockmon's probated will and related documents on file in Los Angeles County archives.

58. IBOP documents, KSUL.

59. Edgar Kaufmann, Jr., *What Is Modern Design?* (New York: Museum of Modern Art, 1950), p. 7. Notions analogous to Kaufmann's occur in the contemporaneous art criticism of Clement Greenberg, who insisted that "a work of art must avoid dependence upon any order of experience not present in the medium per se" (Ilene Susan Fort, "Introduction," *The Figure in American Sculpture: A Question of Modernity* [Los Angeles: Los Angeles County Museum of Art, 1995], p. 8).

60. Ann Kerr, *The Collector's Encyclopedia of Russel Wright Designs,* rev. ed. (Paducah: Collector Books, 1993), p. 159.

61. The display included a ten-inch dinner plate and soup bowl, brown, and a nine-inch vegetable dish and covered casserole, olive green.

62. Brutsche interviews.

63. Box 2, folder 15, IBOP documents, KSUL.

64. Brutsche interviews; and Paul Espinosa, periodic conversations with the author, 1993–94. Espinosa's father, Crescencio Espinosa, had been selling Bauer and other Southern California pottery at their roadside yard in Riverside County for thirty years at the time the plant closed. During those final days they purchased tens of thousands of pieces of speckled Al Fresco and Contempo dinnerware as well as innumerable pallets of unglazed nursery and floral items.

65. Information in this paragraph comes from Chipman, *Collector's Encyclopedia of California Pottery,* passim, and Shotliff, "History of the Labor Movement," p. 345.

66. Shotliff, "History of the Labor Movement," p. 339.

67. Brutsche interviews.

68. Ibid. After the plant closed, several former employees, including Paul C. ("Pappy") Haile and Orville Beckelhymer, submitted a bid of $7,000 to clean up the plants prior to an auction of the equipment and demolition of the buildings. Brutsche permitted them to take master molds from the dump and with the money earned from the cleaning job and the assistance of Tracy Irwin, who made their working molds, Haile and Beckelhymer formed a company of their own, Hailbec Pottery (according to information supplied by Brutsche in a telephone interview 29 September 1994). Their product consisted principally of Irwin-designed florist and garden items in satin-finish glazes of white, black, mahogany, green, and beige. Though the company was not long lasting, the wares do turn up regularly at flea markets today.

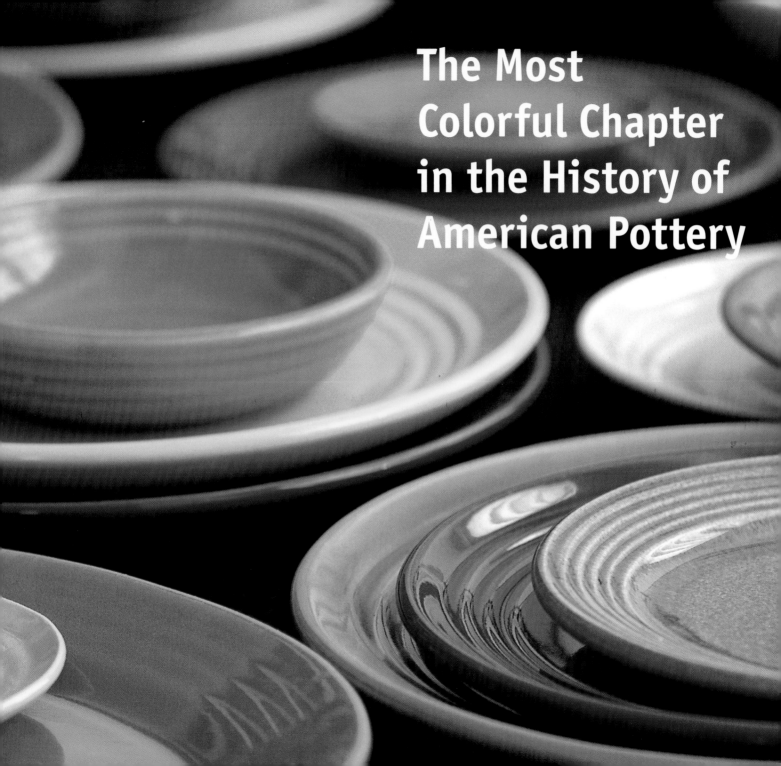

The Most
Colorful Chapter
in the History of
American Pottery

Rebekah Vases

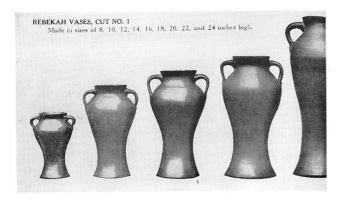

REBEKAH VASES, CUT NO. 1
Made in sizes of 8, 10, 12, 14, 16, 18, 20, 22, and 24 inches high.

Page from J. A. Bauer Pottery Co., Los Angeles, *c. 1915*

Abraham said to his servant . . . "Go to my country and to my kindred, and take a wife for my son Isaac. . . ." Then the servant took ten of his master's camels . . . and went to Mesopotamia, to the city of Nahor. And he made the camels kneel down outside the city by the well of water at the time of evening, the time when women go out to draw water. And he said, "O Lord . . . let the maiden to whom I shall say, 'Pray let down your jar that I may drink,' and who shall say, 'Drink, and I will water your camels'—let her be the one whom thou hast appointed for thy servant Isaac. . . ."

Before he had done speaking, behold, Rebekah . . . came out with her water jar upon her shoulder.

GENESIS 24:2–15

Rebekah jars or vases—the nomenclature was widely shared among potteries early in the twentieth century when Bibles illustrated with Edwardian lithographs were popular—are stately vessels, broad-shouldered, low-waisted, with dramatic handles and only enough of a foot for balance. It's a simple, yet brilliant design, providing an internal well just inside the lip, which deters uncontrolled spillage when the vessel is tipped for pouring.

From its earliest years in Los Angeles Bauer offered hand-turned Rebekah vases, at first in red clay, glazed green or occasionally brown, later in stoneware, and then in glazed earthenware.

Matte Green Artwares

The body of this earliest Bauer art pottery, both hand-thrown and molded pieces, was the iron-rich, red-burning clay mined in Santa Monica and formed daily by machine into tens of thousands of unglazed flower pots. Production of artwares, fired in the same kilns, must have been minuscule by comparison. Body and glaze matured simultaneously in this single-fire process. The glaze had to permit water to evaporate and impurities to evanesce from the clay, and it had to withstand the unpredictable, vaporous atmosphere of the kiln. The result was a deep, matte, mustard-green glaze, porous and sometimes pitted, uneven in texture and density. The clay glows ruddy on the surface.

Improvements, soon in coming, yielded a tighter, more opaque, matte green, capable of achieving a pleasing, silken finish, though not impervious to crazing and crawling. This was, in turn, succeeded by a lustrous, somewhat transparent, still porous, microscopically interwoven blend of greens, with iridescent highlights.

These glazes were applied first to a graduated line of essentially cylindrical vessels and low-profile bulb planters as well as the Rebekah and other vases, bookends, stout jardinieres with lively organic arabesques in low relief, and banks.

Two-fire, high-gloss, lead-glazed stonewares followed. One could simply say the principal colors were blue, green, brown, and black, but that would not do these glazes justice. Formulated without opacifiers, these colors are brilliantly clear and responsive to the sandy clay surface beneath. Each appears as a crystalline colorant afloat in clear glass, the gleaming black in particular revealing its constituent blues and greens. In some the firing produced a glaze that might be described as freckled: blue on pale olive or two shades of tawny brown.

Bauer employees Arthur E. (?) Inglehart, James E. Arblaster, and J. William Eveslage unloading the redware kiln, 1913

Louis Ipsen

No other designer had so long-lasting an influence at Bauer as Louis Ipsen. He is credited with the cast red-clay and stoneware florist items and other artwares of the late 1910s and 1920s, the first tableware of the late 1920s, the company's signature ringware of the early 1930s, as well as the jiggered items in the dinnerware lines—Monterey, La Linda, and El Chico—introduced in the mid- to late 1930s. Victor Houser speculates that Ipsen may have been responsible for the early glazes used on art pottery at Bauer. By the time Houser arrived at Bauer in 1928, Ipsen was the plant superintendent in charge of production.

"He had been pretty well grounded in the pottery business," Houser recalls. "Among other things, he was quite an expert moldmaker. He could create utility designs and floral stuff himself and then make the models, the molds, and put them into production."[1]

Indeed Ipsen's background in the pottery business was extensive (and largely known to us today through the research of Sheryl J. Samuelson).[2] He is said to have worked as a modelmaker in Wisconsin potteries as early as 1891, almost a quarter century before coming to Bauer. His own first pottery enterprise was the American Art Clay Works, cofounded with other Danish immigrants in 1892, but it was short-lived. Ipsen returned to Denmark four years later. By 1903 he was back in Wisconsin, founding the Norse Pottery with his former partner, Thorwald Samson, an artist and ceramic modeler. Their wares were based on ancient Scandinavian bronzes. They exhibited in 1904, as did Bauer, at the Louisiana Purchase Exposition, where they would have seen the by-then ubiquitous matte green glazes of William Henry Grueby and his legions of imitators. They moved the company to Rockford, Illinois, soon thereafter but were producing only a minuscule amount of pottery through 1906. By 1907 Ipsen had departed.

If any general principles can be observed in Ipsen's work at Bauer, they are practicality and adherence to tradition, both aesthetic and technical. In some of his molded artwares one senses the presence of the ghost of Chinese ceramics, whose influence, through centuries of widespread importation, permeated the European manufactories. The bottle-shaped *meiping* is evident in Ipsen's California Vase (PAGE 46, RIGHT); the traditional Yuan-dynasty design of a dragon amidst waves, in his relief-molded jardiniere. His obeisance to traditional craft is found most prominently in the coil-like clay rings of Bauer ringware. The persistence of Bauer themes themselves are apparent throughout Ipsen's dinnerwares, consummated in the short-lived but elegant El Chico line, whose graceful coffee cup, for instance, is none other than the La Linda cup with Monterey rings in ringware colors. La Linda plates are plainware revisited—and rationalized. None of the neobaroque of Ray Murray or the "form follows functionalism" of Tracy Irwin for Ipsen.

The swirl-painting one sees, though infrequently, is almost exclusively applied to Ipsen's molded stoneware line, glazed inside only. Houser reports that when he himself attempted to glaze these stonewares, which had sold poorly on introduction, they were "fired so darned hard that you could hardly get a glaze to stick to them."[3] Swirl-painting, achieved by immersing bisque wares into a bath of oil-based paints floating atop an aqueous solution, may have been an innovative attempt by the Bernheims to make these stockpiled items more appealing.

For all his encyclopedic vision of the pottery heritage, Ipsen was a mensch. Bauer's grandson Bob Sheahan, who worked in Plant One from 1934 to 1940, remembers him as "very cordial, everybody's friend. We all called him Mr. Louis."[4]

He died in 1946.

1. Victor Houser, interview with the author, 5 June 1993.
2. Sheryl J. Samuelson, "Great Danes," *Journal of the American Art Pottery Association* 9 (January–February 1994): 8–12.
3. Houser interview.
4. Bob Sheahan, interview with the author, 16 May 1994.

Matt Carlton

Matt Carlton (in straw boater) on Mount Baldy with (top row, left to right) sons Carlie and Clifton, wife Laura, sons Delbert and Alvie, and (bottom row) daughter Helen and a friend

Toward the latter part of the nineteenth century, Benton, Arkansas, a town of about 1,500, was home to more than a half dozen potteries. Every teenage boy's first job was washing clay or carrying planks of hand-thrown pots to the drying rooms or unloading kilns.[1] Matterson Calhoun ("Matt") Carlton, born nearby in southeast Missouri in 1872, learned to turn pots on the kick wheel by age fourteen. A sometime potter, sometime railroad worker, he married in Benton in 1896, then brought his wife, Laura, and six of their children to Los Angeles in the spring of 1915. Within days he found work as a kilnburner at Pacific Clay Products and joined the community of clay workers living in surrounding Lincoln Heights.[2] It is not known precisely when he went to work for Bauer.

The Carlton family occupied six different addresses in its first ten years in the city before settling on the western slope of Mount Washington. Each morning Carlton walked the two miles downhill to Bauer. Each evening he trudged home carrying clay. At night he molded handles on a piece-rate basis as a way of making extra cash; he had, after all, numerous children to feed.

Collectors generally recognize two distinctive Carlton styles. The first, probably based on earlier Bauer models, includes the stately, symmetrical floral artwares, like the graceful Rebekahs; the towering, cylindrical rose jars (in an array of subtle proportional variations); and the almost conical Venus vases. The second style, which only emerged when Carlton was in his sixties and Bauer had begun applying Houser's sprightly glazes to its artwares, was far more casual, best known for its unmistakably hand-thrown look and spontaneous embellishment. Yet Bob Sheahan, who worked for a time in the 1930s as Carlton's assistant, recalls:

He could make these things all day long, and they looked like they were made in a mold. You could line six of them up, and you couldn't tell one from the other they were so much alike, and he did it all by eye. He was a nice guy, tall and wiry, but he tolerated no nonsense because he was paid by the piece and he was there to make money. He never looked up.[3]

It was as if old age or bright colors had liberated something in the artist, a devil-may-care attitude absent from the meticulous wares of middle age.

In Los Angeles Carlton achieved a minor celebrity. He was seen at the wheel on an Industrial Parade float in 1920, on the pulpit of the Angelus Temple with Aimee Semple McPherson when she delivered a homily on the potter's wheel later that decade, and periodically at the Laguna Art Festival. To this day he can be glimpsed in profile turning clay on the wheel in Frank Capra's film *Lost Horizon*.

Carlton remained at Bauer until 1946. He died at age ninety.

1. Arlene Hyten Rainey, interview with the author, 7 April 1994.
2. Delbert Carlton, interview with the author, 6 April 1994.
3. Bob Sheahan, interview with the author, 16 May 1994.

Plainware

Ringware tea or punch cup

Ringware coffee cup

Monterey

La Linda

El Chico

Al Fresco

Monterey Moderne

Unnamed line

Contempo

Dinnerware

Would that a precise chronology of Bauer tablewares were possible, but with only periodic sales literature, anecdotal evidence, the occasional dated signature on a decorated piece, and the pottery itself to guide us, surmise is often the best we can hope for. We know, for instance, that a new sales catalogue was certainly not published every time a form was added to a line or a glaze was introduced.

We can conclude roughly that Bauer introduced a yellowware dinner service no earlier than 1926—the service does not appear in the catalogue issued sometime that year—and no later than mid-1928, when Victor Houser arrived to find it already in production.[1] Houser first applied colors to those dishes that collectors now call simply "plainware." This unadorned line and ringware, which Bauer itself often described as "ruffled," were marketed together, under the rubric of Bauer California pottery. Nothing more, nothing less. Individual ring items may have appeared as early as 1930, although Herb Brutsche contends that he was present when the first kiln of ringware was unloaded in 1933.[2]

Over the years the shape of ringware was subtly altered. If one were to cut vertically through a dinner plate to view a cross section, it would become apparent that the concavity became increasingly pronounced probably in the late 1930s and again in the mid-1940s. Certain colors are never found on earlier examples; others, never on later examples. This too, when combined with what we can learn about the disappearance of certain glaze constituents at the beginning of World War II and the introduction of glazes formulated to complement new lines after the war, gives some hint of the ringware remodeling dates.

The Monterey line, essentially a series of spheres and circles with flat rims and narrow rings, was among the first to be produced in Plant Two, and that plant went into operation in early 1936. It was followed soon after, perhaps in 1938, by the relatively unadorned and matte-glazed La Linda line. La Linda could be broadly characterized as the hearty plainware refined with a slimmer body made of talc and pastel glazes; La Linda salad bowls nest comfortably within their plainware counterparts. The matte glazes did not meet with popular approval and were joined—and later replaced—by high-gloss substitutes, some in identical pastel shades. The Monterey line was dropped during World War II. La Linda became a staple up through at least the early 1950s. Indeed, as sales literature demonstrates, new La Linda items were being introduced as late as 1952.

Shortest lived of all Bauer lines was El Chico, which probably debuted in 1938, as it appears in a July 1939 price list with a statement instructing customers to disregard earlier advertised prices. El Chico appears as a sort of summation of Bauer's work in dinnerware: the six colors—orange, blue, yellow, green, ivory, and burgundy—are straight out of ringware of the period; the delicate rings, though differently placed, are Monterey; the cup is unmistakably La Linda. The line was gone by the time Bauer issued its illustrated 1941 catalogue.

All of these dinnerwares were the work of Louis Ipsen, supplemented by Ray Murray and perhaps other designers. Monterey Moderne, introduced in 1948, was designed by Tracy Irwin, based in no small part on his work with Brutsche on Al Fresco. It was Irwin, too, who continued to add to Al Fresco once it became a Bauer line in late 1950. Not since the hundred or more items ultimately produced as ringware were there lines as fully developed as Monterey Moderne and Al Fresco.

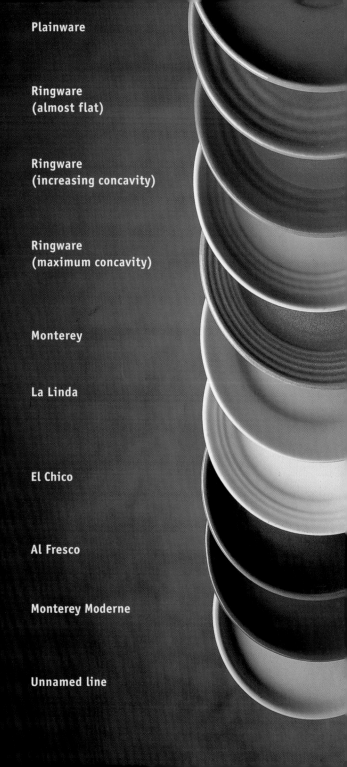

Plainware

Ringware
(almost flat)

Ringware
(increasing concavity)

Ringware
(maximum concavity)

Monterey

La Linda

El Chico

Al Fresco

Monterey Moderne

Unnamed line

Al Fresco with a face-lift—new matte earth tones—became Contempo around 1960-61. Sometime prior to that a new, never-christened line of almost severely geometrical dinnerware was developed and permitted to languish. Given their present rarity in the pastel, speckled glazes of the 1950s, their slightly more common occurrence in the Contempo colors of the early 1960s, and Brutsche's failure to recall them as clearly as he does the bulk of production after his return to Bauer in late 1960, it is possible that their debut was about 1958-59.

1.   Victor Houser, interview with the author, 5 June 1993. A white-glazed set consisting of six hand-thrown mugs and a jug and six mold-made saucers, painted with lovebirds, signed "c.s.f.," and dated March 1, 1928, appeared on the market in October 1994.
2.   Herb Brutsche, interview with the author, 11 March 1994.

"What's So Mexican about El Chico?"

Of Bauer's so-called Spanish pot, one of many glazed garden items, John Miali, for twenty years a commissioned sales rep, confesses, "I never saw anything Spanish about it."[1]

Was there anything authentically Latin American about the Bauer line, or was the romance of sunny Mexico a fad, a fancy, a merchandising ploy?

Despite the company's presence at the 1915-16 San Diego fair, showcase extraordinaire of the Spanish colonial revival style, not a single Spanish name appears in the c. 1915, c. 1919, nor yet the c. 1926 Bauer sales catalogue, save for its Montecito vase, named for an upscale Santa Barbara suburb. Then throughout the late 1930s and early 1940s—the decade of *The Cisco Kid* and *Romance of the Ranchos* on the radio; "Mañana" and "South of the Border" on the jukebox; *The Gay Desperado, Juarez, The Mark of Zorro,* and *Mexican Hayride* on the silver screen—came the Monterey (RIGHT), La Linda (CENTER), and El Chico (LEFT) lines (not to mention Gladding, McBean's Cocinero, Coronado, and El Patio; Haldeman's Caliente; Homer Laughlin's Fiesta; Metlox's Pintoria; and Pacific's Coralitos).

Some argue that at least Bauer's saturated hues were derived from glazed Mexican tiles,[2] but there's just as much evidence that Mexican ceramic crafts of the day were made in imitation of American decorative foibles. Witness the drowsing peons and art deco-influenced shapes of much tourist pottery. All of this takes on a certain irony when one considers the significant proportion of Bauer's labor force that was Mexican by birth or ethnic origin.

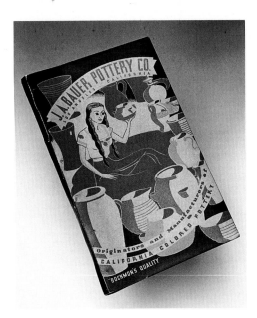

Sales catalogue, c. 1939

1. John Miali, interview with the author, 5 September 1994.
2. For a refutation of this and other well-meaning attempts to link Southern California dinnerwares with authentic Mexican material culture, see James Oles, "South of the Border: American Artists in Mexico, 1914-1947" in *South of the Border: Mexico in the American Imagination, 1914-1947* (Washington, D.C.: Smithsonian Institution Press, 1993). For example, "For many visiting Americans, Mexico was distinguished by its vibrant, tropical colors, a recurring theme recorded in innumerable travel accounts. Color not only expressed Mexico's difference from New York or Berlin; it also symbolized an intensity of life and opposition to the grays and blacks of machine age existence, made even more dreary by the Great Depression. Like the popular Fiestaware of the 1930s and 1940s, [Josef] Alber's [painting] *To Mitla* [1940] distilled Mexico down to dramatic color and an allusive name" (pp. 167, 170).

Victor Houser

Mr. Topping wanted a set of nested mixing bowls he could whole-sale for a dollar. A salesman at Morton Pottery, he turned to the company's twenty-two-year-old ceramic engineer, a 1927 graduate of the nearby University of Illinois, and urged him to perfect colored glazes that would be attractive to homemakers yet adapted to economical one-fire manufacturing. Victor Houser gave him green, light blue, and yellow.[1] Thus sunny Illinois, not sunny Mexico, ultimately became the birthplace of the modern Bauer palette.

Houser remained only briefly at Morton, moving to Southern California in the spring of 1928. After several months at a failing tile shop in Whittier, he was hired by the Bernheims to develop colored glazes at Bauer. He recalls:

I don't know exactly what they expected of me. All I know is what I was able to develop for them under the circumstances. I had some formulas that I had used at the tile place and at Morton.

The glazes that we started using at Bauer were commonly known as lead glazes. Those glazes could be fired at a considerably lower tempera-ture than glazes with smaller amounts of lead and other ingredients. We weren't making the colored items in near enough quantity to fill a kiln, so they would set red clay up so high and then did what we called topping out with the colored stuff. That red clay had all the impurities and moisture that you have in an unfired clay, and all those fumes didn't do the glazes a darned bit of good. So I had to develop a glaze that would withstand that as best it could. It was kind of a hit-or-miss thing, experimental, and when you got one that worked, why, that was fine.

We used all raw glazes at that time, all raw materials. Lead was probably the principal one, and there was feldspar and quartz, or silica, all ground up real fine. Then there were zinc oxide and tin oxide. The tin was an opacifier. Cripes, you could buy it under fifty cents a pound then. We'd buy it by the barrel. If you didn't put that in, the glaze was transparent. You put this tin oxide in, maybe 6, 8, 10 percent, depending on the color, and that would make it about the same shade as if it was heavy and drip-ping. Of course, I didn't like my glazes to drip.

First Houser made jade green, delph blue, and Chinese yellow, followed shortly by black, white, and California orange red, though it's no longer possible to say just when or in what order. When the Monterey tableware line was introduced, its deep blue was added to the ringware line as well, as were ivory and burgundy. For Mon-terey Houser also developed a lighter yellow, a redder orange, a speckly brown, and turquoise.

At Plant One we never changed from the original stoneware body, which is fired to about cone 7 or 8 and pretty near impossible to fit to all the glazes. When the body and the glaze have different coefficients of expan-sion, you're going to get some crazing, if not right away, then eventually, after weeks or maybe months. At Plant Two we used a talc body fired at a much lower temperature but better suited to putting these colored glazes on. If both were fired right, you didn't have any crazing for years and hopefully never.

At Bauer the salesmen to have an edge were always wanting something different. They wanted different finishes too. The color wasn't as hard to achieve as the degree of satinness. In time the matte finish became desirable, and that's how the La Linda dishware pattern came about.

First sold in six matte pastels—green, blue, yellow, cream, pink, and peach—the matte finish was soon eliminated with the line reintroduced in an almost identical set of glossy shades, but for honey brown in place of peach. Houser's final color sequences were developed (freelance) for Brutsche's Al Fresco dinnerware—in green, chartreuse, gray, burgundy, and brown—and for Bauer's derivative Monterey Moderne in variant tints of these plus pink, black, yellow, and eventually off-white.

The precise names of many of these along with other colors appear in various Bauer sales catalogues—reprints of some have been published by and for collectors; photocopies of others pass from hand to hand—but such publications never kept pace with the proliferating hues. No sooner does a reader conclude that a palette was restricted to a particular set of shapes than examples of all the "wrong" shapes in all the "wrong" colors appear, as do colors for which there are no names at all: a light, bright papaya orange; no fewer than a half dozen pale blues and blue-grays; and an elusive russet, perhaps the rarest of all.

Yellow, orange, green, and Monterey blue were the most popular colors. Light blue was least popular. Very little white was made, a little more black.

Originally I made my own colors, my own yellow stain. I would buy some commercial colored stains and blend them with pure minerals. We used quite a variety of inorganic minerals. The maroon-red was a calcine of chrome and tin. Black was usually a mixture of two or three ingredients; cobalt and probably manganese. Eventually you could buy a prepared black stain, and it wasn't any more costly than buying the ingredients separately, so I'd just put that into my glaze. Of course, you couldn't use the same base for all these colors by any means. The one you used to make the uranium orange was nothing much more than lead carbonate, silica, a little clay, and uranium.

You've probably run across variations and whatnot. Lack of close quality control accounts for a lot of it. We made the colors at both plants, and it's quite possible that I used different formulas. Different firing time, different firing conditions, maybe a little variation in the glaze. It could be a variety of things. Then, of course, you might just get hold of an experimental thing that they never made much or sold very much of.

Houser's job consisted of more than developing glazes. He was constantly involved in monitoring their application and firing. During World War II he was the superintendent of Plant Two as well. In the early 1950s he left the company and along with a fellow employee, Robert ("Bob") Redd, he formed his own pottery, Alvi, making floral and novelty items. When Redd fell ill, Houser sold out to his distributor, Jaru Art Products, and continued producing pottery for them for another twenty years.

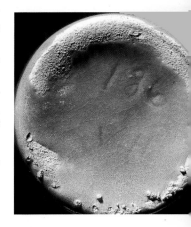

Glaze test (note the initials V. H.)

1. Much of the information and all the quotations in this and the following section come from the author's interview with Victor Houser, 5 June 1993, and subsequent telephone conversations.

The Color Orange

California would be unthinkable without the color orange, radiant, ubiquitous symbol of its climate, abundance, and promise. Orange was not the first glaze color that Houser developed, but it is surely his most memorable achievement. Bauer orange, or "California orange red" as it was called in sales literature, is simply more vivid than the corresponding hues created by other potteries, largely because it was unadulterated by opacifiers and, even to the naked eye, appears subtly three-dimensional. The not-so-secret ingredient was uranium, purchased by Bauer in significant quantities in the form of an oxide known as sodium uranate.

Uranium has been in use as a ceramic colorant since its discovery in Joachimsthal, Germany, in the early nineteenth century. There it was found that minute quantities of uranium salts—hardly more than traces—imparted shades of yellow, orange, brown, green, and black to ceramic glazes. Uranium's versatility was the subject of widespread research by the American Ceramic Society early in this century. Hardly a color could not be coaxed from compounds of uranium and other elements, though cheaper means to almost every desired glaze, with the exception of orange, were generally available.

The oranges on Brayton and Catalina pottery may have beat Bauer to market. These were opaque and occasionally iridescent. Houser's orange was, by contrast, essentially transparent: microscopic, highly colored particles suspended in a clear, faintly amber, vitreous lead. This is most apparent along rims or where rings rise like reefs from a pool of dark, syrupy glass. In places the body ceramic itself peeks through.

John Twilley, art conservation scientist at the Los Angeles County Museum of Art, analyzed several samples of Bauer orange. He set his findings in a clearly comprehensible scientific context.

In general the decorative and protective glazes applied to ceramics may consist of two kinds. In the first they may be comprised entirely of a glass, colored or colorless, which is fused to the body of the ceramic. In the second there may be one or more nonvitreous (nonglassy) ingredients suspended in the fused glass.

Color in a completely vitreous glaze arises from some highly colored compound dissolved into the glass. Most of the intensely blue cobalt glazes are of this type. In the partially nonvitreous glaze an undissolved crystalline material remains suspended in the glass. If uncolored, it may simply serve as an opacifier, helping to cover the body ceramic from view by scattering light inside the glaze. If colored, it acts both to hide the body ceramic and to contribute to the total color of the glaze. Bauer orange is of this type.[1]

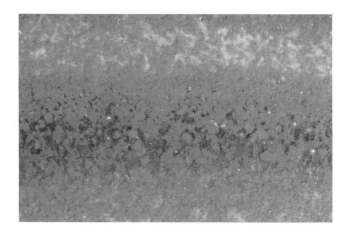

Sample of Bauer orange-red glaze photographed 3.4 times life size

The other principal constituents of the glaze were water, silica (that is, clay), and lead. "Pure lead," Houser recalls. "Boy, these glazes had a lot of lead in them. Lead in itself will make a yellowish glaze. If you left all the uranium out, with that amount of lead in there it would have been a kind of pale yellow. If you overfired it a little bit, or it was a little bit heavy, it would tend to separate, and you would have orange flakes in a kind of a clear matrix."

Given the popularity of its orange-glazed items, Bauer had a standing order with its chemical suppliers for about 450 pounds of Congolese sodium uranate every week. In 1942, with the Manhattan Project under way, the government interdicted the commercial use of uranium and its oxides—despite the fact that the sodium uranate used in the ceramics, glass, and photography industries was largely depleted, that is, without the highly charged U-235 isotope that made the element critical in the development of atomic weaponry. All Bauer orange items (with the exception of the pumpkin color introduced in the early 1960s) can therefore be dated to 1942 or earlier. (The government did not restore uranium to commercial use until 1958.)

Is the uranium in these items dangerous to collectors? We think the lead may kill you first.

Houser experimented, roasting the raw material before mixing the glaze: "With uranium you got a very limited range of orange colors, but I found that by calcining this uranium compound—putting it in a sagger [heat-resistant ceramic pan] and putting it in the kiln and firing it—you would get a deeper shade. I think the reason was, some of the sodium probably evaporated when you fired it the first time. So I did that, and I got a deeper orange than some of the others got."

Twilley considered Houser's procedure: "Often the production of a certain color requires some control of the atmosphere in the kiln. Precalcining the colorant can protect this process from the vagaries of the atmosphere inside the kiln heavily loaded with vessels, some of which may be differently glazed."

1.   This and all other quotations from John Twilley derive from his undated manuscript, "Technical Analysis of Bauer Glazes and Related Materials" [1994], which he generously prepared especially for this occasion. The slide (PAGE 60) is also his.

Fred Johnson

For perhaps a quarter century before coming to Bauer, Fred L. Johnson had been an accomplished thrower at Niloak Pottery in Benton, Arkansas. He worked at founder Charles Hyten's wheel, turning, as did the other potters,[1] shapes that conformed to the Niloak catalogue. Indeed, in silhouette numerous Johnson pieces made at Bauer are almost indistinguishable from their Niloak counterparts.[2]

A substantial, balding figure, well into middle age, Johnson left Benton, accompanied by his wife, Lota Mae, daughter, Theda Lee, and son, James R. ("Jimmy"), soon after Hyten sold the company in 1934. Both Fred and Jimmy were at work at Bauer by about 1936 (they made their first appearance in the Los Angeles city directory in 1937), the elder Johnson at the wheel in Plant Two, his son by his side, working as his helper, smoothing his pots with a sponge and carrying them to the drying room. Unlike the Matt Carlton pieces, which are almost never glazed on the bottom, Johnson's

sometimes are. These were fired with a dry foot; perhaps Jimmy carved them.

Compared with the flamboyance of Carlton's later work, Johnson's is the very model of restraint. The sign of his hand lingers only on the inside of each turned piece, some of which were later adapted to slip casting and perpetuated for years through molds.

It is likely that Carlton himself had something to do with the Johnson family's decision to come to Los Angeles. Johnson was Carlton's nephew, the son of his sister, Beulah. When the Johnsons did arrive,

Jimmy and his wife, Anna, lived across the street from the Carltons on Roseview Avenue; Fred, Lota, and Theda lived on the same street, just a block and a half down the hill.

Johnson's tenure at Bauer seems to have been but a moment. His name appears only three years in the city directory, though Lota, Theda, Jimmy, and Anna remained. A Fred L. Johnson died in Los Angeles in November 1940. Jimmy stayed at Bauer until just months before the final closing. He worked as Victor Houser's assistant in the glaze department, and when Houser left, he became chief glaze chemist. The speckle pastel and matte earth-tone glazes of the 1950s and early 1960s were his.

We tend to think of just two potters at Bauer laboring away in their somewhat antiquated fashion—Carlton at Plant One, Johnson at Plant Two—but there were more. No fewer than three wheels were turning at Plant Two, with Johnson making his floral items, Gaetano Miali and a man named Brown, their garden pots and sand jars, the tallest of which were created in two cylindrical sections, later joined with slip. For a time Miali created the jardinieres to which molded lions' heads and swags were sprigged with slip.[3]

1. Arlene Hyten Rainey, interview with the author, 7 April 1994.
2. David Edwin Gifford, *The Collector's Encyclopedia of Niloak* (Paducah: Collector Books, 1993), passim.
3. John Miali, interview with the author, 5 September 1994.

Ray Murray

Gloss Pastel teapots

There are certain cars that resemble Bauer teapots. The 1947 Hudson is one; the 1950 Mercury, another. This is not entirely coincidental. When I asked Ray Murray if Aladdin's lamp had been his inspiration for the now eponymous teapot, he said, "No, speeding down the boulevard." When I confessed that Hudsons of a certain vintage evoke that teapot for me, he admitted gleefully that he'd owned one, a 1947.[1] The earlier of the two designs, however, was his; the Gloss Pastel teapot first appeared in the Bauer sales catalogue of June 1941.

In less than four years with the company—December 1937-October 1941—Murray was responsible for an astonishing number of designs. An art major at the University of Oklahoma, his initial experience with pottery had come through odd jobs: mixing and kneading clay for ceramics students and cleaning their studio, where John Frank, owner of Frankoma Pottery, was teaching. After graduation in 1935 Murray went to work for Frank, remaining a year or so until Frankoma had trouble meeting the payroll. (The company's dancing Indian warrior and Chinese heads are Murray designs.)

Lack of capital in Washington, D.C., foiled his plan to go into the pottery business there on his own, and by December 1937 he was in Los Angeles, working at Bauer Plant Two. The modernity of the facility, with its tramways and tunnel kilns, impressed him. He took his turn at the wheel beside Fred Johnson. He cut templates for the jiggers used on the Monterey line. He cast liquid clay in molds. Shortly thereafter he was training with Louis Ipsen, modeling and cutting plaster for molds.

Murray's earliest designs were additions to the Monterey line. In production since 1936 at Plant Two, Monterey consisted solely of jiggered table items—plates, cups, bowls—all essentially circular or spherical, designed by Ipsen. By June 1938 Murray had added slip-cast pieces—a covered butter dish, platters, a gravy boat—all essentially oblong, but with rounded corners, followed soon by an even greater departure, a miniature sugar and creamer set, all sharp, intersecting angles, sharing little with the remainder of the line except its bands of fine, densely packed decorative surface rings.

He undertook similar modifications to the exceedingly restrained La Linda jiggered tableware, and by July 1939 it too included slip-cast pieces, identical in form to his Monterey items absent the rings. By contrast, his gravy boat—perhaps he already had his eye on the boulevard—surges forward, its flared and elongated spout balanced by a giant scorpion's tail of a handle (PAGE 57).

And then there is Cal-Art, a line of lightweight, slip-cast, matte and later high-gloss florist items, designed to look complicated—fluting, spiraling, torquing, bowing (art deco by way of the neobaroque)—but engineered to be simply and cheaply built. Murray recalls his goal was "an inexpensive ware as decorative as possible in a production way: the designs were all bold, and the molds wore for a long time. We didn't try any fine artwork. The only gluing was the handles." He had to bear in mind "what the casters were

Ray Murray designed items in the Cal-Art line

capable of, and at Bauer they weren't terribly experienced people. Notice everything is pretty broad, the fluting, for example; we didn't try anything but these bulky type things." To his flat centerpieces were added a series of novelties to be placed among flowers: streamlined, nearly abstract Madonnas and animal figurines. Murray contributed the diminutive hippopotamus. Then there were his swan-shaped planters, six, eight, and thirteen inches long, naturalistic, yet elegant.

The Cal-Art line was a collaborative, ongoing effort, with pieces added and others eliminated. Murray's glazed swirl flower pots and jardinieres, with vertical ribs spiraling clockwise, then doubling back, remained in production to the very end.

Even with Cal-Art to his credit, Murray's designs for Gloss Pastel Kitchenware were his most deceptively simple and longest lasting. Sometimes referred to by collectors as the wedding-ring

pattern, each item—the teapot, capacious ball pitcher, stout cookie jar, and homey nesting bowl set—is encircled with broad, protuberant bands increasing or decreasing in width from base to rim. Appearances aside, the engineering was sophisticated. The teapot, made not for today's tea bags, but for loose tea, is a marvel. After steeping, tea can be poured without a strainer; not a leaf goes up the spout. To clean, swirl hot water in the pot and dump it out; every leaf flushes quickly away.

In 1941 Murray moved on. He left Bauer and went into business making ceramic costume jewelry. In 1944 he was drafted. After the war he worked with Miramar Ceramics and later freelanced. Today he lives in Hawaii.

1.   Much of the information and all the quotations in this section come from the author's interview with Ray Murray, 2 May 1994.

Hand-decorated Bauer

The painted Bauer one finds is as likely to be the work of professionals as that of amateurs. China painting and other hand-decorating of ceramic forms was so popular a pastime in the 1920s and earlier that every issue of *Keramic Studio,* a journal addressed to professionals and nonprofessionals alike, contained detailed patterns to be copied, complete with suggested color schemes. Among those contributing was Helen V. Carey, a Los Angeles china painter with a studio in the flatlands of Hollywood. There on Bauer yellowware—nesting bowls and bean pots—she painted her vivid, somewhat awkward blossoms and trailing vines in orange, green, terra-cotta, and gold. The Depression was unkind. After years in her private studio, she was forced to earn her way as a retail clerk and later a stenographer. She disappears entirely from the city directory in the mid-1930s. Could she have died then of a broken heart?

The signature of Harry Bird, best known for his work at Vernon Pottery, can be found on Bauer ringware. Ona M. Blunt painted subtle florals. Hope Sandoval (whose father, Crescencio Espinosa, began selling Bauer from a pottery yard in Prado, California, in 1933 and until his death in 1994 at 101 went to work each day at his pottery yard in Loma Linda) painted mission scenes on the bisque seconds her father bought in job lots and trucked home in his 1927 Ford pickup.[1] Walt Klages maintained a studio, decorating Bauer and other brands with overglaze painting of strawberries and rural kitsch. Other names—Hoylockey, Kuykendall, Southern California watercolorist Mary Jean Lloyd, and Powell among them—appear as well.

The benefit to collectors of all these decorated pieces, apart from being lovely, embellished objects to enjoy, is that they were often dated and sometimes provide evidence of the surprisingly early introduction of certain forms.

1. Hope Sandoval, interview with the author, 28 September 1994.

Crescencio Espinosa and family, c. 1940s. Hope Sandoval stands third from left. While most of this decorated pottery is not Bauer, certain items, such as Bauer's swirl flower pot, are clearly visible.

Bauer's Russel Wright Line

With revelers thronging the city far below, tooting horns and embracing loved ones—or anybody handy—Herb Brutsche spent the evening of V-E Day (May 7, 1945) with Russel Wright on the terrace of his Park Avenue penthouse, toasting the Allied victory over Germany with champagne. Wright and Brutsche had come to an understanding regarding a line of Wright-designed ceramic decorative and gift items to have the appearance of handcrafted artwares but be manufactured by Bauer in Atlanta.[1]

Despite Brutsche's determination to abandon tablewares, kitchenwares, and the florist trade, he realized that, lacking priorities for such strategic materials as brass and rubber, it might be some time before he could convert the plant from military production to sanitary wares. "I knew if we had to go back into jiggering those doggone plates again, we couldn't beat Fiesta or any of the automated plants to the north of us. I was looking for a line that was going to be unique, and Russel Wright in my estimation was a modern man. Wright's American Modern was the hottest dinnerware line in the business. I was sold on the guy. I called him up one day and talked with him."

Not that Wright himself was unaware of Bauer Pottery and its accomplishments. A mid-1930s promotional photograph of Wright's spun aluminum line includes as a ceramic accent Bauer's remarkably successful plainware carafe.

"I said to him, 'I'm interested in developing a modern artware line.' Just simple as that," Brutsche recalls. "A certain amount was for his work, his designing; I think I paid him $5,000 or $6,000 for that. Beyond that he was to be on a royalty basis."

Anyone who's ever attempted to wash the inside of an American Modern teapot or carafe knows that eye-catching design, not practicality, was Wright's strong suit. That flaw carried over to the Bauer project. Individual objects weighed in at over five pounds of fired clay; the gondolalike centerpiece, two feet long and four inches wide, weighed eight pounds, six ounces. Explosions in the kiln resulted. The bubbly silica glazes, astonishingly ambitious, were equally troublesome. The "molten" glass would drain down the sides of the objects and adhere to the slabs beneath, creating unsalable seconds and even thirds. In Brutsche's succinct words, "It was murder."

The line of twenty objects was introduced in early 1946. Of Bauer's six hundred accounts, only one ever reordered. The company lost about $65,000 on the venture.

Today, of course, the agony of defeat long forgotten, many of the Wright pieces look nothing less than visionary: biomorphic, substantial, and to the degree that their subtly combined, lavalike coatings express the hellish temperatures of the kiln, consistent with the modernist dictum of faithfulness to process and materials. The items, when found, are among the most costly of Bauer collectibles.

Russel Wright spun aluminum table accessories in a setting designed by Mary Wright

1. Much of the information and all the quotations in this section come from the author's interview with Herb Brutsche, 1 May 1994, and various telephone conversations.

An interesting account of the relationship between Bauer and Wright appears in Ann Kerr, *The Collector's Encyclopedia of Russel Wright Designs*, rev. ed. (Paducah: Collector Books, 1993), pp. 119–25.

Brusché Lines

The Dixie Sanitary line established, Herb and Virginia Brutsche returned to Los Angeles in 1947. As predicted when they left for Atlanta eight years earlier, Herb Brutsche had indeed acquired "a million-dollar education back there."[1] He had visited the biggest potteries of the Midwest and witnessed the benefits of automation. He had sold the Bauer Atlanta line into prestigious East Coast department stores, worked with Russel Wright, kept his "finger on the pulse" of the consumer. In the West ringware sales were declining, and Brutsche was keen to see Bauer modernize, automate, keep abreast of the times, but his mother-in-law, Eva Bockmon, and her nephew, plant manager Jim Bockmon, were not. She simply would not invest the capital; he seemed satisfied with current production.

With a rented plant on land owned by Rose Hills Cemetery in Whittier and a new automated jiggering machine, the first on the West Coast, Brutsche went into production with Al Fresco, an entirely new dinnerware line. "I knew what the boys were doing back East. I knew what was selling, and I had this idea of making a contemporary ware, as far away from the ringware as you could get."

The conceptualization, inspired by the success of the American Modern coupe shape, was Brutsche's: plates that were flat as the proverbial pancake but for a brusque concavity at the rim; bowls with sides that rose steeply from flat bottoms; serving pieces with simple profiles and sharply angled handles. Tracy Irwin produced the master molds; Victor Houser, the glazes. "That green," Brutsche recalls, "was more or less a number from Mary Wright," whose proposal for a line of dinnerware to be produced by Bauer Atlanta had met with little enthusiasm. "That bottle green of hers? Mine had a little more life to it." Al Fresco was introduced in just four colors: green and chartreuse, maroon and gray—compatible pairs. By the time of the 1950 Museum of Modern Art exhibition in Chicago, brown had been added. These were the colors of the day, made

Al Fresco (Brutsche Ceramics)

Al Fresco (Bauer Pottery)   *Contempo*

popular in drapery and upholstery fabrics, evoking a tropical paradise. "That's where I got the ideas." Along with the new line came the new phonetic spelling—Brusché—in ads that tersely rhymed, "Say Broo-shay."

Mangle driers Brutsche had bought from Mt. Clemens for use on the Navy bowls and tumblers had been idled in Atlanta by the conversion to sanitary ware. Brutsche brought them to Whittier. Unfortunately, they arrived disassembled, costing months of precious labor. Still, the line, once introduced, fared well. "I had good customers in New York City. I had Carson Pirie in Chicago. I had Gimbels and Wanamakers's in Philly. I had the best in all those towns. Bullocks did the same for me in Pasadena [as Sears had done for Bauer during the 1930s]. I pushed and pushed."

Suddenly, in March 1950, Rose Hills announced plans to refurbish its property, and in June Brutsche was forced to move. Again there were six weeks of costly downtime while the plant was relocated to Glendale. The precious weeks lost to the transition were crippling. In the fall of 1950, with the MOMA exhibition still installed in Chicago, Brutsche Ceramics ceased as a sole proprietorship and was merged into Bauer. Brutsche retired from active management.

Jim Bockmon continued the Al Fresco line, first in the Monterey Moderne glazes, then in speckled pastel glazes developed by Jimmy Johnson. When Brutsche returned as general manager of Bauer in late 1960, the line was repackaged as Contempo with a new set of matte glazes.

1.　Much of the information and all the quotations in this section come from the author's interviews with Herb Brutsche, 11 March and 1 May 1994, and various telephone conversations.

Made in the 1950s: Bauer's Late-Period Artware

Jack Chipman

A s the J. A. Bauer Pottery reached the midcentury mark, the higher-ups must have paused to reflect on their company's glorious past. Were they also bemoaning the fact that the Los Angeles firm was slipping as a ceramic industry trendsetter? Bauer, after all, had been *the* originator of California colored pottery,[1] but this was the early 1950s, and the tide definitely seemed to be turning.

It was up to Tracy Irwin, Bauer's leading designer at that time, to help maintain the firm's competitive edge. Irwin's previous work in completing the popular Cal-Art floral line and the recent introduction of his Monterey Moderne tableware had resulted in his having an esteemed position within the company. His contributions in the 1950s were no less impressive as he applied a design philosophy inspired by none other than the leading American industrial designer, Russel Wright.[2]

The purchase by Bauer of the Cemar Potteries at about midpoint in the decade complicates any assessment of Bauer's late-period artware. I suspect the buyout came about in part because this rival business had been the brainchild of two of Bauer's own employees, Paul E. Cauldwell and C. J. Malone.[3] What's intriguing is the possibility of a preexisting similarity in the art lines of Bauer and Cemar. Is it simply in retrospect that the two lines seem to integrate so well, or could Irwin have moonlighted at Cemar in its early days as he had at Brutsche Ceramics?

Bauer designs of the 1950s that can be securely attributed to Tracy Irwin more often than not look good alongside the additions made from Cemar molds. His standouts include the Indian bowl made in two sizes, the pumpkin bowl also made in two sizes, the minimalist compote with matching candleholders, and the dome pot made in many sizes with three-legged, black or brass-

plated stands to match. The dual purpose pedestal pot, which could serve as jardiniere or, inverted, as pedestal, and the angular vase, which essentially combined jardiniere and pedestal in a single cast form, are typical of the spare, "less is more" Irwin style.

Another side of the designer occasionally surfaced in a tendency toward the bizarre. These three cast vases, each made in eight- and ten-inch sizes but unfortunately unnamed in sales literature, illustrate his slightly eccentric leanings.

Among the Cemar-turned-Bauer items is an interesting assortment of leaf-shaped vases and other floral items, ranging from the wispy, four-inch vase to the much larger and more fanciful vase, which was available at up to thirteen inches. All came in three of Jimmy Johnson's speckled glazes—lime green, pink, and oyster white—translucent, high-gloss finishes containing minute metallic flecks.[4] Although not a Bauer exclusive (Cemar itself had utilized them), Bauer made very good use of this type of glaze not only on floral and garden lines but on kitchenwares and tablewares as well. An apparent Bauer innovation was the rather garish addition of 14-karat gold sprayed over the upper portions or outer edges of some glazed forms in the late 1950s.

The other principal artware finish of the period was a very solid, satin, matte glaze. Colors included muted tones of green and brown in addition to white and the outstanding black. Forms receiving these glazes were also sometimes subjected to the gold overspray.

Successful holdover designs from previous years were produced in either muted solid or speckled colors. I suspect the classic Biltmore jardiniere was an early Irwin creation. This and other Irwin designs were carried in stock right up to the time the company closed.

An accounting of the artware produced near the end of the Bauer era inevitably leads to a comparison with the company's previous glories. The Depression years are generally considered the firm's golden age in both tableware and artware output. In a valiant attempt to keep pace with the swollen ranks of local producers and to stem the tide of postwar imports, however, Irwin and his associates left a fitting final legacy in the Bauer artware they made in the 1950s.

1. In sales catalogues published in later years, Bauer boastfully claimed itself the "originators and manufacturers of California colored pottery." This was probably true, even though Catalina Clay Products of nearby Santa Catalina Island could have legitimately laid claim to the distinction too.

2. The influence of Wright on Irwin's design for Monterey Moderne is possibly less evident than it is in the forms he modeled after Bauer assumed production of the Brusché line.

3. Cemar Potteries, located at 3024 Rosslyn Street, produced a variety of floral artwares, novelties, and kitchenwares, beginning in September 1935 and continuing to the mid-1950s.

4. The company's October 1, 1959, catalogue "Florist and Garden Pottery by J. A. Bauer Pottery Co., Manufacturers of Clay Products" lists four other speckle colors: turquoise, yellow, brown, and gray.

Ten Bauer Pottery Collections

Ben S. Wood III
Jugs

"Most jug collectors are interested foremost in what's on a jug: the proprietor's name and the town in which he operated. Probably 90 percent of all advertising jugs were liquor jugs—distillers, distributors, and saloonkeepers—although there are jugs for druggists and vinegar companies. Collectors naturally like jugs from different towns, small towns, towns that are no longer in existence. A lot of times you can get some idea that certain jugs came from the same pottery either by the way that they're stenciled or the particular printing scratched in the glaze. You certainly can connect a lot of jugs to the J. A. Bauer pottery in Paducah by means of its particular block capital font. Bauer seemingly sold its jugs far and wide, as we have seen printed examples from as far southeast as Savannah, Georgia, and as far south as New Orleans and certainly Mississippi, Alabama, Tennessee, and Kentucky. I am not personally aware of how many of their jugs went north, although I do have some Missouri examples, and I believe I also have some Illinois examples.

"Sometimes, though not very often at all, you also find the pottery maker's mark. I only have one example. It has 'J. A. Bauer, Maker, Paducah, Ky.' debossed on the shoulder and then in scratch lettering 'Go to Knight's Palace Saloon at the Railroad Crossing, Fulton, Ky., for Fine Liquors.'

"When I started out, I was only going to buy Hopkinsville, Kentucky, jugs. Then as the hunt went on, and I could see that that wasn't really going to satisfy my appetite, because I was finding so few, I decided I'd collect not only Christian County jugs—Hopkinsville is located in Christian County—but any county touching Christian County. That evolved into anything from western Kentucky, and that evolved into Kentucky, and then it became anything in Kentucky and Tennessee because some of my ancestors came from Tennessee. Now I've expanded again because jugs are so hard to find; I collect jugs from anywhere in the south and west.

"I think the escalating value of these jugs has made some of them come out of the woodwork. Back when they were in the $10-25 range, people weren't real excited about looking in their attics, because $10 or $25 didn't mean that much. Now that jugs are up probably to a minimum of $100 and bringing as much as $200, $300, $400, and $500—some of the real rare ones—that's caused a lot of people to say, 'Well, I believe I would,' especially those for whom the $500 means a heck of a lot more than the jug. I've got close to 1,600 jugs today, and yet if I started now, I'd be well to probably have about 100 jugs in my collection. There'd be no way I could own this number starting at today's prices.

"Jug collecting is a little bit of like being a detective. It's the hunt that's the real thrill, seeking out a jug with a name on it that no one else has seen before. The collectors swap information with each other—we call each other and ask, 'Have you ever seen this jug before?'—but we probably all hold back information from each other also. It's kind of rubbing your friend's nose in the dirt a little by showing him, 'Look what I've found.'"

Clare Graham and Bob Breen
Indian Bowls

GRAHAM: "The first Indian bowls we bought, we bought because of the shape. They look like Prairie School architecture with those little glyphs on the side, the way that those are built in. So we just started buying because of that recurring motif. Of course, there are a lot of Indian bowls that aren't necessarily Bauer, but gradually as these things accumulate, you start noticing that the better-proportioned ones are marked 'Bauer' on the bottom. Then you start noticing the engraved numbers, and it becomes a matter of getting each of the variants and gradations. The numbers refer to sizes, probably the diameter at the top. Like an '8' has an eight-inch diameter. Higher numbers are larger sizes.

"The Bauer Indian bowls that are marked are all slip cast; you can see mold lines on them obviously. The big ones we have, which are hand thrown, have another kind of tab, a blocklike, attached tab [rather than the more graceful, angled tabs on the slip-cast Bauer bowls]. Bauer may have actually thrown the large bowls also, but because they were hand production, they were never marked on the bottom. In a mold you have the signature and the number. The problem with Indian pots, if you have a number 10 and you get another number 10 and another number 10, there's not a unique distinction between them, because it's production-line stuff.

"Unfortunately Indian bowls have become vogue among Arts and Crafts collectors as the outdoor accompaniment for Arts and Crafts and California bungalows. Anybody who collects Stickley furniture, when they have pots around, they are these. We rarely buy them now because the prices are up. Anyway I think it's something we have enough of. We have too many. Of course, if there's a different size or a different shape or a different color in glaze…But we have them now in redware and glazed and some bisque white. They're all outside except the glazed ones. Outside they have bromeliads in them. The ones inside have dice and anagrams and Scrabble tiles and other things that are accumulating until they turn into something else." [1]

1. For an idea of what that something else might be, see the interview with Graham in *Magnificent Obsessions: Twenty Remarkable Collectors in Pursuit of Their Dreams* (San Francisco: Chronicle, 1994), pp. 83-87.

Mark Wiskow and Susan Strommer
Matt Carlton Vases

WISKOW: "The first thing you ought to have in the Bauer book is a section on what isn't Matt Carlton. I've seen people who ought to know better, serious Bauer collectors and /or dealers: a bowl that ought to be 22 bucks, they'll have $295 on it or $195: 'rare Matt Carlton form.' Uh-uh.

"Part of it is availability. You know how it is: people want to go out on Sunday and come home with something or at least see an example that, if it didn't have a chip or wasn't marked $800, they could buy. They want to participate. You go to a pottery show, and there's some of what you collect. And we're not unaware that since we started with Matt Carlton, it's rocketed in value, and that's always positive reinforcement.

"We don't actually know anything about Carlton personally."

STROMMER: "He hasn't really entered into our interest as a person, only as an identifier."

WISKOW: "In fact, I'm not sure what the appeal of his pottery is."

STROMMER: "The colors, of course."

WISKOW: "The colors, and the fact that it's handmade rather than molded. You keep discovering new shapes. My goal was to get the armed ones, which seem to be everybody's favorite, but I think we had ninety-two pieces before we got the four ascending sizes in the four basic colors. For some reason green and orange, especially in that shape, have eluded us. We've got four yellows, three cobalts, but green and orange we only have one of each.

"Part of what I like about the pieces is that they are unique. Even the pieces that are supposed to be the same aren't; one's got close rings, another's got rings spaced farther apart. Another thing I like about the handmade is they're easy to use. The wavy lips, for example, like the ones on top of the cupboard: flowers fall wonderfully into each of those little nooks and just look great. Some of these other bigger pots have very small mouths, so you don't need ninety dollars worth of flowers."

Paul Preston and Tim Lukaszewski
Monterey Moderne Dinnerware

PRESTON: "We started out with yellow, deep yellow. Yellow was the color that we both were very attracted to, and that was what we went for for a while. We needed some dinnerware. We didn't have any dinnerware, and we went for yellow, and then we expanded to red. I don't remember how this went exactly, but we had seen or heard about black, and there was some hesitation about getting into it, because it seemed like it would be an impossible one to find."

LUKASZEWSKI: "There's so little of it, we thought we would never get a set together."

PRESTON: "And then we didn't know whether each pattern or size or shape was, in fact, made in black. Burgundy seemed comparable to yellow. But black? It was harder to find. We weren't always sure. Did they make a ten-and-a-half-inch plate? Did they make salt and pepper shakers? Did they make a sugar bowl? In fact, they did, but not everybody had the same story when we were hunting around: 'Oh, no, of course, they didn't make it in black.'

"My first reaction to chartreuse was, 'God, what a strange color.' Then, after I sort of sat with it for a while, I really liked it, so we kind of decided, 'OK, we'll go to the fourth color.' Now we have all the other colors. That was a very devious plot on Tim's part. Somewhere along the way he said . . ."

LUKASZEWSKI: "'Pink.'"

PRESTON: "He was going to collect gray and pink and olive, but he was going to keep them in the basement."

LUKASZEWSKI: "So then we just had to have some brown too."

PRESTON: "And extra cabinets built for the other colors."

LUKASZEWSKI: "It's no fun having stuff in boxes."

PRESTON: "We've gone through about thirty states, as far as Ohio, through Texas and New Mexico. Our biggest haul was in Texarkana, but mostly it's been piece by piece from flea markets, street fairs, and antique shops, sometimes tucked away on little bottom shelves, sometimes in glass cases. The prices we pay vary dramatically, sometimes extremely cheap and sometimes not so cheap."

LUKASZEWSKI: "We set as a goal—a very strange goal—service for twelve in each color, and we're all done. Now, it's fun looking for the hard-to-find pieces. We'd like to get a burgundy canister, and there are a couple of more states that we haven't seen."

PRESTON: "We really do enjoy spending our spare time going off for the day, sometimes for the weekend, to this antique show or that little town and prowling around."

LUKASZEWSKI: "Plus all the stores close at five, and then you have the whole evening, so it really works out well."

Linda Dodge
Swans

"I really can't remember which one I found first—either the larger yellow one or one of the chartreuse—but I do remember that when I saw it, I just thought it was the most perfect representation of a swan, especially the gracefulness of the neck. That's really amazing. When I kept seeing them more and more in other colors, I thought, 'Gee, I've got to have a whole flock.' Each one was so unique and so beautiful in its own right. I just wanted them all together.

"I've been buying them now probably six or eight years, and I've passed up a few that were really outrageously expensive. I don't think I've paid more than forty-five or so. Of course, we're always searching for the black swan and the maroon, the burgundy swan."

"Do you know if there are burgundy swans?"

"I've never seen one."

Jimm Edgar
Animals

"Some people have expressed doubt that these animals were made by Bauer, but that unknown factor has become part of the intrigue. In collecting Bauer animals, we move from the known to the unknown. The hippo (CENTER, REAR) and the Scottie (LEFT, FOREGROUND) are the only ones illustrated in Bauer sales catalogues. So we're confident about them. The ducks no one seems to have questioned; they come in glazes—matte blue, satin green, yellow, and others— that correspond to Bauer colors. The next step is to identify animals with the same clay and glaze treatment. Then they become unmistakable too.

"The next animal that I discovered was the horse. The clay and glaze are exactly the same as the hippo and Scottie. Then came the discovery of the horse mounted on the Bauer plant coaster (CENTER). It's apparent that this was done in the factory and confirms the horse and the process. I suppose someone could have brought a horse into the factory and fused it to a plant coaster, but that's even more difficult to believe than the opposite.

"So we went from the known of the hippo and Scottie to the horse and felt we were doing the right thing. Then the collie and lion were discovered. Again, they were the exact same clay and glaze, and you have to make a deduction, but it seems reasonable. It's like finding a piece of Matt Carlton; you go by the glaze and the clay.

"The little duck with the big bill (FOREGROUND) was confirmed by Jack Chipman's observing them in Tracy Irwin's home. You can put that duck up against any Bauer Cal-Art pink, and it's the same glaze. You conclude it is Bauer. The little angel fish (LEFT, CENTER), again, is the same, and you make the same deduction.

"An advanced collector must pick areas of focus or become overwhelmed. Some people focus on dinnerware, and I have some rare pieces myself, but my focus has become Matt Carlton and the animals. At some point you have to begin to be selective. I recently sold all my black ringware plates—I just don't use them—but it's a source of pride for me having collected these animals, particularly the horse on the plate."

David Murphy
Speckle Ware

"Display is my profession, so it was easy for me to look at these pieces, at the relationships of depth, height, and color, and pull it all together. I've got the pieces pretty well divided according to a possible marketing scheme: the kitchenware, the serveware, the florist ware, the artware. From a visual point of view, this room may actually be more massed out than a Bauer factory showroom, with all the pieces I've accumulated. It's probably a little too much for a retail display too. That would have a lot less pieces. There would not be the multitude of colors in each shape. You would just find the one that would be complementary to the whole scheme.

"I found my first few pieces of speckled Bauer at a flea market when I lived in Salinas, California, in the early eighties. I had a great set of Fiestaware at that point, which included a lot of the 1950s demitasse cups and saucers and very hard-to-find pieces. Collecting Fiestaware, you're out at the flea markets, you're out at the antique shows and the shops, so you do see other makers. I knew Bauer was a great collectible, but it was just the curiosity of finding the pastel colors. I got hooked by paying maybe five or six dollars for eight or ten pieces, including a coffee pot. I was selling other collectibles at that time and tried to sell some of the speckle, and nobody wanted it, so I kept it.

"I used to have a lot of art deco, the big, heavy Egyptian or oriental-type motifs, and the Fiestaware is more of the thirties vintage; it had the bright colors and art deco rings. When I decided I was tired of the thirties and wanted to move up a couple of decades, I wound up in the atomic 1950s in furnishing, and I thought that the speckle ware would enhance that.

"It's art to me. It's an accumulation of design and of an era in America and what was popular. So I don't use it. I just enjoy looking at it. Every once in a while, if I'm entertaining, I'll drag out one of the more modern pieces and set it up for decoration. One dinner party I served off all pink speckle ware. That's when I had gray chrome dining room chairs and table, and it was really pretty.

"It's amazing how routinely I find 'the one piece I've never seen before.' I guess I may have the luck of the Irish, of walking in and seeing that piece. Of course, if you collect something for as long as I have, you can see it a mile away. If you're looking over an entire booth, you focus on that one item and hone in on it real easily. That's how I found an eleven-inch pink speckle ashtray, even though it was halfway buried."

FRAGILE DO NOT DROP

BAUER
No.450 2-QT. CASSEROLE & COVER
COLOR
TYPE FRAME

Michael Brashier
Oil Jars

"My children. I consider these oil jars my children, and I treat them as children. I care for them, and they bring a lot of love and a lot of life to our environment. They bring a lot of charm. They're a great design and the only Bauer line that I focus on.

"One jar standing alone can be a statement, but a cluster of jars puts off a different feeling. It gives you so much more life. That's the bottom line. It gives you more life.

"I got interested in the oil jars because of our home. Terry [Freed] and I bought a Spanish home that was in horrible need of repair, but it had a lot of great iron on the windows, the kind of planters that you pop colorful little pots into. Unfortunately I took those planters off because I hated them originally. Nevertheless I came to recognize that colorful pottery can be important in getting your house to work. Terry had begun collecting Bauer dinnerware, just buying a piece here and there and throwing it on the shelf. I started thinking the colors were incredible, so I asked, 'Why don't we try using this in the rest of the house?' The oil jars fascinated me most because of their size and unique design. Subsequently, I learned a lot about them.

"The design was taken from a utilitarian jar used for packing table oil in the 1700s and 1800s. Back then people would buy a barrel of wine or a large jar of oil, and that would be the supply for a year. Often the jars had spigots. Bauer's design was taken from those oil jars, but it became gardenware, as far as Bauer was concerned.

"Basically there are two styles: the no. 100 and the no. 129. The 100 has a more pronounced, rounded 'doughnut' at the top and more of a belly-type shape. They are closer in spirit to the original utilitarian design. No. 100 was available in 12, 16, and 22 inches. The rarest is the 12 inch, and it is most often found in Chinese yellow. Occasionally it's seen in jade green or red-orange. Cobalt, delph blue, black, turquoise, ivory, and white are extremely rare in the 12 inch. My most recent discovery is the maroon. With the 16 and 22 inch you most often find turquoise and green.

"No. 129 is generally known in two sizes: 20 and 24 inch. The 20 inch you usually find in turquoise and green and occasionally red-orange, cobalt, and yellow. I have one in black, and I've never seen another. When you get to the 24 inch, it is almost always red-orange; any other color would be rare.

"There is actually a 9 inch no. 129 oil jar. I have two. It could be that the little jar was simply top-heavy, and that's why so few survive.

"There was a lot of very average stuff in Bauer's line, and there's a gross amount of very average stuff on the market. Only about 20 percent is considered perfect. The other 80 percent is cracked, chipped, flawed, usually scratched, and that makes it inferior. A lot of collectors, due to the way this stuff has increased in price over the last few years, can't afford to focus on perfect stuff, but I think if they pay $10 or $15 for a less than perfect plate, they've wasted their money. If you stay focused, however, you can put the best of the best together. If you stay focused, your Bauer fantasy will become reality. My goal is an oil jar in every size in every color, and the challenge is going to continue until I meet that goal."

Mitch Tuchman
Bisque

I have, I contend, the world's worst collection of Bauer: few, if any, of the rarest pieces of ringware, far from the greatest number of Carlton vases, exactly two Indian bowls. My Monterey Moderne, such as it is—mostly olive green, a bit of chartreuse, three or four pieces of burgundy (one crazed), no black to speak of, one yellow—I use every day.

The history of the company interests me, however, so I've collected items representative of all its lines. Even more intriguing are the anomalies, objects that simply shouldn't exist, pieces that never appeared in sales catalogues: kitchenware in red clay; iridescent, slip-glazed bean pots; a two-tone ringware cup; a twice-glazed Ipsen molded vase, outside Houser green, inside Ipsen blue. The weirder, the better, as far as I'm concerned. A cunning dealer once called out to me, "I have ugly Bauer today." He had—now I have— a jade green ring tumbler freckled with congealed lumps of some once-molten metallic substance.

To the degree that I specialize, bisque is my passion. There are two varieties: pieces that were intended to remain bisque—the dismally unsuccessful Ipsen line of artwares that are glazed blue, green, or brown on the inside, left unglazed outside—and seconds.

Bauer sold seconds on wooden pallets in job lots, the prices arbitrarily set by the salesmen in the yard. Pottery yards bought bisque for quick turnaround. Amateurs bought it to decorate. I buy it because I love it. The shapes are pristine; their details, crisp; their marks, brilliantly legible. A mysterious aura surrounds each piece with its pathetic, untold story of perceived imperfection and callous disregard. I take them home and give them a good scrub and find them a spot among others of their kind, where the vain hierarchies of rare glazes never intercede.

Sharalynn Mahoney Greene
Ringware and Flower Pots

"Bauer speaks to me of California as I was growing up. Being born in Pasadena and living in Los Angeles, it seemed to me that Bauer was an old friend, something that I had been surrounded by my entire life. My mother and grandmother used Bauer garden pots—they were always around—so when I started my Bauer collection, it was a collection of all the colors of garden pots. Of course, it didn't end there. One item begat another. Then the goal was everything in ringware from the 1941 sales catalogue, as impossible as that may seem.

"Maybe this sounds too noble, but collecting Bauer is like saving a part of California's magnificent past. We look at the people who created Bauer, people like Victor Houser, Matt Carlton, and Fred Johnson whose names are readily identifiable as artisans now when in truth they were just people doing a job. It shows how a job can become a creative endeavor and that people can create something that is truly magnificent and unique and have everlasting value."

Selected Marks

Debossed mark found occasionally on slip-glazed Paducah Pottery stonewares

Debossed mark found on redwares

Cobalt-stenciled mark in use until c. 1920 on Bristol-glazed stonewares

Debossed mark found on poultry founts, mid-1920s

Debossed mark found on a wide range of table and kitchenwares, early to mid-1930s

Cobalt-stenciled mark introduced c. 1929

Special debossed mark found only on carafes

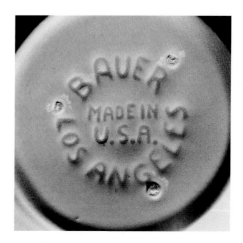

Debossed mark found on a wide range of table and kitchenwares, from the mid-1930s onward

Debossed mark found on the Monterey line

Gummed, foil-paper label, 1930s (?)

Debossed mark found on Gloss Pastel kitchenware

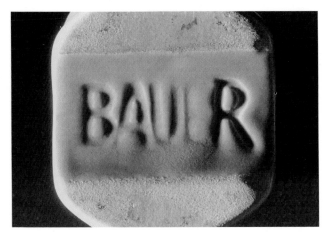

Debossed mark found on some Cal-Art items

Debossed mark found on some Bauer Atlanta items

Cobalt-stenciled mark found on U.S. Navy items

Debossed mark found on Russel Wright items

Debossed mark found on Al Fresco items made at Brutsche Ceramics and later at Bauer

Debossed mark found on some artwares, 1950s

Debossed mark found on some artwares, 1950s

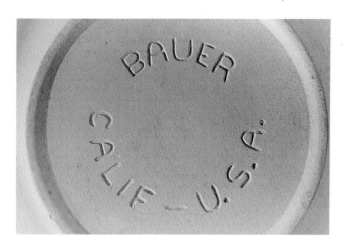

Debossed mark found on unnamed dinnerware line, late 1950s and/or early 1960s

KITCHEN AND TABLE POTTERY
2-FIRE GLAZED
PRICES IN EFFECT JANUARY 1st, 1939

J. A. Bauer Pottery Co.
W. E. BOCKMON, Prop.

Manufacturers of

CLAY PRODUCTS   Net List

Bockmon's Hi Grade Stoneware, Flower Pots, Garden Pottery, Art Pottery, Tiles
415-421 West Avenue 33   Phones CApitol 4204-4205   Los Angeles, Calif.
This list supersedes all previous lists. Prices subject to change without notice.
Packing charge varies approximately from 2 to 5% according to assortment packed.
The goods listed below are carried in stock in Jade Green, Delph Blue, Chinese Yellow, Black,
Monterey Blue and California Orange Red.
See our seven price lists for prices on all kinds of pottery.   For illustrations see Catalogue.

Wholesale Each		Retail Each		Retail Each	Wholesale Each
	PITCHERS			**PLATES (RING)**	
.25	No. 12 1½ Pt., Ruffled	.50	No. 61 9 In. Dinner Plates ....$ .50		$ .25
.40	No. 12 1 Qt., Ruffled	.80	No. 61 10½ In. Dinner Plates ... .80		.40
.55	No. 12 2 Qt., Ruffled	1.10	No. 62 7½ In. Salad Plates...... .32		.16
.75	No. 12 3 Qt., Ruffled	1.50	No. 63 6 In. Bread and		
1.00	No. 13 3 Qt., Tall Dutch	2.00	Butter Plate.................... .24		.12
1.00	No. 14 3 Qt., Low Dutch	2.00	No. 63 5 In. Bread and		
.30	No. 16 1 Pt.....................	.60	Butter Plate.................... .20		.10
			No. 64 12 In. Chop Plate 1.20		.60
	CUP and SAUCER (Plain)		No. 64 14 In. Chop Plate 1.70		.85
$ .25	No. 17 Plain ....$	.50	No. 64 17 In. Chop Plate 2.50		1.25
	PLATES (Plain)		**SERVING or SALAD BOWL**		
$ .25	No. 18 9 In. Dinner Plates ....$	.50	**(RING)**		
.40	No. 18 10½ In. Dinner Plates ...	.80	No. 65 9 Inch.................$ .70		$ .35
.16	No. 19 7½ In. Salad Plates......	.32			
.12	No. 19 6 In. Bread & Butters	.24	**SOUP PLATE (RING)**		
$.75 Dz.	No. 20 4½ In. But'r Chips, Dz .	1.50	No. 66 7½ Inch.................$ .40		$ .20
	No. 21 SPICE JARS RUFFLED		**SOUP OR CEREAL BOWL**		
Each		Each	**(RING)**		
$ .30	No. 1 4½ x 3½ Inches............$	.60	No. 67 4½ Inch.................$ .25		$ .12½
.40	No. 2 6 x 4½ Inches.............	.80			
.60	No. 3 6¾ x 5¾ Inches.............	1.20	**SALAD BOWL (RING)**		
$ 1.30	PER SET ....$	2.60	No. 68 9 Inch.................$ .80		$ .40
			No. 68 11 Inch..................... 1.20 .60		
	No. 25 COFFEE SET		(Can be used for Pretzel Bowl)		
1.80	Complete	3.60			
.50	1 Qt. Pitcher.....................	1.00	**PUNCH BOWL (RING)**		
.15	4 Oz. Mugs........................	.30	No. 69 14 Inch.................$ 2.00		$ 1.00
.40	10 In. Tray	.80			
			PUNCH CUP (RING)		
	No. 26 TUMBLERS		No. 70 ....$ .20		$ .10
$ .10	3 Oz., Ruffled.................$	.20			
.12	6 Oz., Ruffled.................	.24	**GRILL PLATES**		
.15	12 Oz., Ruffled.................	.30	No. 71 8 Inch.................$ .60		$ .30
			No. 71 10 Inch................. 1.00		.50
$ .50	No. 27 3 Pt. Water Jug, Ruffled .$	1.00	No. 72 12 Chop Plates,		
.20	No. 29 12 Oz., Plain	.40	Plain 1.20		.60
			No. 72 14 In. Chop Plates........ 1.70		.85
	No. 30 BEAN POTS				
$ .20	1 Pt., No Handle ....$	.40	**PLATTERS**		
.30	1 Qt., 2 Handles	.60	No. 73 9 In., Ring .... .60		.30
.40	2 Qt., 2 Handles	.80	No. 73 12 In., Plain or Ring ...$ 1.00		$ .50
.50	3 Qt., 2 Handles	1.00	No. 74 Sugar Bowl, Plain .... .50		.25
.60	4 Qt., 2 Handles	1.20	No. 75 Creamer, Plain .... .50		.25
	(We do not make Bean Pots in		No. 77 4 Inch Baking Dish and		
	Orange Glaze.)		Cover (Ruffled................. .30		.15
			Separate Dish .... .20		.10
	BEATING BOWLS		Separate Cover .... .10		.05
$ .25	No. 31 4¾ x 5 Inches, Ruffled....$	.50	No. 78 3½ Inch Ramekin,		
			Plain, Dozen ....$ 1.50		$ .75 Dz.
	No. 32 PUDDING DISHES		No. 79 Salt or Pepper Shaker,		
$ .12	No. 1 5½ Inches Wide ....$	.24	Ring, each .... .40		.20
.15	No. 2 6¼ Inches Wide	.30			
.20	No. 3 7½ Inches Wide	.40			
.30	No. 4 9 Inches Wide	.60			
.40	No. 5 10 Inches Wide	.80			

No. 34 CUSTARD CUPS

$ .75 Dz. Ruffled ....Doz. $ 1.50

CASSEROLES AND BAKING DISHES

$ .35	No. 36 6 x 3 Inches, Ruffled ...... $	.70
.60	No. 36 6½ x 3¾ Inches, Ruffled..	1.20
.75	No. 36 7 x 3¾ Inches, Ruffled....	1.50
	No. 37 Batter Bowl, Ruffled,	
.50	2 Qt...........................	1.00
.35	1 Qt. (Gravy Bowl)............	.70
	No. 37A Beating Bowl Pitcher,	
.35	5 x 5 Inches, Ruffled...............	.70

CEREAL BOWL, RUFFLED

$.20 No. 38 6 Inch ....$ .40

HONEY JAR, RUFFLED

$.35 No. 39 14 Oz.......................$ .70

CREAMERS and SUGARS

.25	No. 40 Sugar Bowls, Ring..........	.50
.25	No. 41 Creamer, Ring............	.50
	No. 42 Midget Sugar Bowl,	
$.20	Plain or Ruffled ....$	.40
	No. 43 Midget Creamer, Plain	
.20	or Ruffled	.40
.20	No. 44 12 Oz., Ruffled...........	.40
.15	No. 46 8 Oz., Plain	.30
	No. 47 Refrigerator Set, Ruf-	
.60	fled, Complete	1.20
.15	6 x 2½ Separate Container........	.30
	Separate Cover	.30

DRIP COFFEE POT (RUFFLED)

$ .85 No. 48 8 Cups ....$ 1.70

INDIVIDUAL COFFEE POT PLAIN

$ .30 No. 49 2 Cups ....$ .60

TEA POTS

$ .35	No. 50 2 Cups, Ruffled ....$	.70
	No. 50 6 Cups (Ruffled or	
.60	Plain)	1.20
	No. 51 6 oz. Tumbler for Raffia	
$ .12	Wrapped Handle ....$	.24

FRUIT DISH

$ .12 No. 53 5 Inch ....$ .25

OVAL VEGETABLE DISH

$.60 No. 54 10½ Inch ....$ 1.20

CUP and SAUCER (RING)

	No. 59 Ring Coffee Cup and	
.25	Saucer	.50
	No. 60 Ring Tea Cup and	
$ .20	Saucer	$.40

No. 80   MIXING BOWLS

No. 36	1 Pt. Ring.............	$.20		.10
No. 30	1½ Pt. Ring.............	.30		.15
No. 24	1 Qt. Ring.............	.36		.18
No. 18	1½ Qt. Ring.............	.46		.23
No. 12	½ Gal. Ring.............	.56		.28
No. 9	1 Gal. Ring.............	.80		.40
PER SET, 9 to 36 Inclusive ....$		2.50	$	1.25
No. 6	1¼ Gal. Ring............$	1.24	$	.62
No. 4	1½ Gal. Plain............	1.40		.70
No. 3	2 Gal. Plain............	1.70		.85
No. 2	2⅞ Gal. Plain............	2.00		1.00
No. 1	3½ Gal. Plain............	3.80		1.90

PEDESTAL BOWL

No. 81 14 Inch ....$ 3.00 $ 1.50

SALAD BOWL

No. 82 12 Inch ....$ 1.30		$ .65
No. 82 14 Inch 2.00		1.00

SHERBET or ICE CREAM DISH

No. 83 Plain or Ring ....$ .40 $ .20

GOBLET

No. 84 Plain or Ring ....$ .50		$ .25
No. 86 10½ Inch Relish Dish.....$ 1.20		$ .60
No. 87 Coffee Server, Plain....... 1.50		.75
No. 87 Coffee Cover.............. .30		.15
No. 88 Low Salt or Pepper		
Shaker, each .... .35		.17½
No. 89 3 Oz. A.D. Cup and		
Saucer.......................... .40		.20
No. 90 Nappies —		
5 Inch ....$ .30		$ .15
6 Inch .... .36		.18
7 Inch .... .50		.25
8 Inch .... .60		.30
9 Inch .... .80		.40
PER SET ....$ 2.30		$ 1.15
No. 91 Sugar Shaker .... .60		.30
No. 92 Berry Dish .... .20		.10
No. 93 6 cup Coffee Server,		
Ruffled, ... 1.80		.90
No. 94 8 cup Coffee Server,		
Ruffled, with Metal Handle		
and Cover 1.80		.90
No. 95 6 cup Tea Pot, with		
Wood Handle................. 1.50		.75
No. 96 Covered Butter Dish ......$ .64		$ .32
No. 97 Pickle Dish.............$ .60		$ .30
No. 98 Cookie Jar ....$ 1.20		$ .60
No. 99 Gravy Bowl ....$ 1.00		.50

METAL ACCESSORIES

$ .10	No. 26 6 oz. Tumbler Handle .....$	.20		
.10	No. 26 12 oz. Tumbler Handle ...	.20		
.10	No. 51 6 oz. Raffia Wrp. Hndl ...	.20		
$ .10	No. 34 Custard Rack.............$	.20		
$ .12½	No. 78 Ramekin Rack ....$	.25		
.20	No. 36 6 In., Cassa Frame	.40		
.25	No. 36 6½ In. Cassa Frame	.50		
.35	No. 36 7 In., Cassa Frame	.70		
$ .20	No. 47 Refrig. Jar Frame	.40		
$ .15	No. 64 10 In. Chop Plate			
	Handle.............................$	.30		

No. 64 12 In. Chop Plate				
Handle ....$		.30	$	.15
No. 139 Holder for 4 Ash				
Trays ....$		.20		.10
No. 154 Holder for 4 Ash				
Trays		.20	$	.10
Fluffy Beater ....$		.20	$	.10
Ice Bowl Holder ....$		.20	$	.10
Ice Tongs		.10	$	.05
Salt and Pepper Holder ....$		.20	$	.10
No. 42, 43 Sugar and Cream				
Holders ....$		.30	$	.15

Suggested Retail Price List.

No Allowance for Freight or Breakage.

Prices F. O. B. Factory.

Acknowledgments

Had it not been for the generous invitation of artist and pottery historian Jack Chipman, I would never have presumed to write this book. Jack was coauthor of *The Complete Collector Guide to Bauer Pottery* (1982), the revered early Bauer study, now long out of print. He had been contemplating a revised edition and weighing the demands of that effort against his desire to devote a greater proportion of his time to painting. I had recently published a reprint of the c. 1919 Bauer sales catalogue and just finished writing *Magnificent Obsessions: Twenty Remarkable Collectors in Pursuit of Their Dreams,* when, one Sunday in March 1993, Jack suggested that I undertake writing the history of the J. A. Bauer Pottery Company afresh. I accepted the challenge, and Jack promptly lent me his considerable collection of Bauer sales literature. Throughout the research and writing of this book he has continued to share his knowledge.

Many others offered invaluable assistance, permitting me to record their reminiscences, making research materials available, or lending objects from their personal collections of Bauer pottery for photography. They are all acknowledged here gratefully.

John Herbert Brutsche, who during his long association with the Bauer Pottery Company was universally known as "Herb" and only subsequently revealed his preference for "Johnny," sat through two long interviews and innumerable telephone calls. His astonishing memory almost invariably stood the test of corroboration. The voice of corroboration was often that of Victor F. Houser, whose own memories from several decades as Bauer's chief glaze chemist and ceramic engineer were especially illuminating.

Similarly generous with their time and trust were three of J. A. Bauer's grandchildren: Dorothy Hilton, daughter of Katie Bauer; Bob Sheahan, son of Mayme Bauer; and the late Dallas Speers, Jr., son of Tillie Bauer. Their enthusiasm for this project was most gratifying.

Several whose generosity was manifested over and over again deserve special recognition. These include Michael Brashier and Terry Freed (On the Twentieth Century, Pasadena), Jeffrey Dangermond, Naomi Murdach (Naomi's Antiques to Go, San Francisco), and Doug Stanton. All are collectors and, not coincidentally, dealers. (Naomi once asked me if I knew the difference between a collector and a dealer. The answer, he told me, is thirty minutes.) Denny Burt demonstrated his commitment to the project by arranging numerous loans of pottery from the collection of the late Buddy Wilson. He also led me to Paul Espinosa of La India Pottery Shop in Loma Linda, California, undoubtedly the largest repository of items actually purchased directly from Bauer Pottery itself. The story of late Bauer can hardly be studied without repeated journeys to Loma Linda.

Finally, there is Robert Evans, a gentleman devoted to the history of Paducah, Kentucky. Fortunately he appointed himself my tireless guide and permitted no stone to be left unturned. Sadly he died before the project was completed. This book is dedicated to his memory.

In addition I wish to thank the following:

In Arizona
Karen Innes

In Arkansas
David E. Gifford
Arlene Hyten Rainey

In California
Leslie Greene Bowman
Bob Breen
Delbert Carlton
Jewell Carlton
Vincent Crisboi,
    Los Feliz Florists,
    for flowers on PAGE 23
Anne Diederick
Linda Dodge
Dean Doser
Jimm Edgar
Crescencio Espinosa
James Field
Glenna Ford
Van Fryman
Clare Graham
Sherry Greene
Paul Lenaburg

Gary Levasser
Tim Lukaszewski
Charles McDougal
Frank Miali
John Miali
Jack Moore
Darcy Morris,
    Golyester, for the fabric
    backgrounds on PAGES
    70–71
David Murphy
Gail Nelson
Paul Preston
Maureen Russell
Joe Ryan
Hope Sandoval
Phil Sheridan
JoAnne Speers
Bill Stern
Susan Strommer
Nancy Thomas
John Twilley
Dan Walters
Buddy Edward Wilson
Mark Wiskow

In Colorado
Marion Speirs

In Hawaii
Ray Murray

In Indiana
Jeanne Burke
Rev. Bruce A. Strotman

In Kentucky
Anthony Barnes
Mrs. James Bauer
Kathryn Biatcher
William Black, Jr.
Earl Cron
Dick Holland
Ed McDermott
Nettie Oliver
Ben S. Wood III

In Ohio
Paul Farace

Index

"Every woman in
Southern California
knew Bauer"

JOHN HERBERT BRUTSCHE

Audrey Hepburn on the set of *Sabrina* (1954)

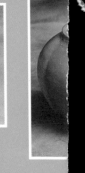

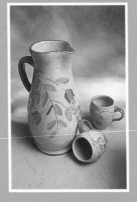